Tiny Habit Shifts

Step-by-step Guide to Building Good Habits and Developing Atomic Habits for Personal Transformation

Sean Harper

Table of Contents

Preface

In a world that moves at a relentless pace, the pursuit of professional excellence can often feel overwhelming. We're bombarded with advice on making radical changes, achieving monumental goals, and transforming ourselves overnight. But what if the secret to unlocking our fullest potential lies not in grand gestures, but in the smallest of actions?

Welcome to "Tiny Habit Shifts: Step-by-step Guide to Building Good Habits and Developing Atomic Habits for Personal Transformation". This book is born from the understanding that lasting change doesn't come from sporadic bursts of effort, but through consistent, intentional adjustments to our daily habits. The journey to professional success is not a sprint; it's a marathon composed of countless, deliberate steps.

Throughout this book, you will learn to identify the habits that currently shape your professional life, both the beneficial and the detrimental. You will discover how to align these habits with your career goals, ensuring that every action you take moves you closer to the excellence you aspire to achieve. We will guide you through the process of making tiny, manageable shifts in your habits, demonstrating how even the smallest changes can have a profound impact on your performance and satisfaction at work.

Our approach is grounded in the latest research on habit formation and behavioral science. We believe that by focusing on small, incremental changes, you can build momentum and create sustainable improvements. This book is not about drastic overhauls; it's about making subtle yet powerful shifts that accumulate over time to produce significant results.

As you embark on this journey, you'll find practical strategies, real-life examples, and tools to help you track your progress. Each chapter is designed to be actionable, providing you with clear steps to take as you work toward integrating new habits into your daily routine.

Whether you're at the start of your career or looking to reach new heights in your professional journey, "Tiny Habit Shifts" is your guide to unlocking the power of small changes. By the end of this book, you'll not only have a deeper understanding of how your habits influence your professional life but also a concrete plan for making those habits work for you.

Thank you for choosing to invest in yourself and your future. Let's begin this journey of transformation, one tiny shift at a time.

Sincerely,

Sean Harper

Introduction:

The Power of Tiny Habits

Understanding the Impact of Small Changes

In the quest for professional excellence, it's easy to get caught up in the allure of dramatic transformations and overnight success stories. However, the most profound and enduring changes often stem from small, consistent actions. This concept is beautifully illustrated by the story of the British cycling team's remarkable journey to success.

In 2003, British Cycling was far from the dominant force it is today. In fact, their performance was so lackluster that professional cycling brands refused to sell bikes to them, fearing it would hurt their reputation. Enter Dave Brailsford, who was appointed as the new performance director. Brailsford pioneered an innovative approach later recognized as the "aggregation of marginal gains."

He believed that by breaking down all aspects of bike riding and improving each by 1%, the cumulative effect of these small gains would lead to a significant overall improvement. This approach wasn't just about training and strategy; it extended to every possible aspect of the cyclists' lives.

Brailsford and his team made numerous tiny changes: they redesigned bike seats for more comfort, used alcohol to clean the tires for better grip, and taught riders the best way to wash their hands to avoid infections. They even brought in a surgeon to teach the athletes how to avoid infections by proper hand-washing. These changes might seem trivial on their own, but together, they created a powerful cumulative effect.

The results were staggering. Within five years, the British cycling team dominated the 2008 Beijing Olympics, winning 7 out of 10 gold medals in track cycling. They continued this dominance in the 2012 London Olympics and also achieved unprecedented success in the Tour de France, with British cyclists winning the race multiple times.

Why Tiny Habits Matter ?

The story of British Cycling highlights the remarkable impact of small habits. Each small change, while seemingly insignificant on its own, contributed to a massive overall improvement. This principle isn't limited to sports; it can be transformative in any professional field.

When you concentrate on making small, incremental changes in your daily habits, you lay the groundwork for lasting and sustainable growth. These tiny adjustments are not only simpler to introduce into your routine but also easier to sustain over the long term. This ease of implementation helps prevent feelings of overwhelm or burnout that often accompany more significant changes. Consequently, your likelihood of achieving long-term success is greatly enhanced. As these modest changes become a consistent part of your life, they begin to add up. This gradual accumulation results in noticeable and substantial enhancements in your overall performance and productivity.

By focusing on small but consistent habit shifts, you ensure that your progress is steady and sustainable, leading to meaningful and lasting improvements.

The Science Behind Habit Formation

Understanding the science behind habit formation is crucial for making effective and sustainable changes in your behavior. Habits are created through a process called "chunking," where the brain consolidates a series of actions into an automatic routine. This automation process is driven by a three-step loop consisting of a cue, a routine, and a reward.

Cue: This is the initial trigger that initiates the habit. It acts as a signal to the brain, indicating that it should start the habitual behavior. Cues can come in various forms, such as a specific time of day like waking up in the morning, an emotional state such as feeling stressed, or a particular event like finishing a meal. These triggers are essential because they set the habit loop into motion.

Routine: This is the behavior or series of actions you perform in response to the cue. The routine is the actual habit itself and can range from simple actions like brushing your teeth, to more complex behaviors like exercising. When the cue is encountered, the brain executes this routine almost automatically, as it has been programmed to do so through repetition.

Reward: This is the positive reinforcement you get after finishing the routine. The reward is crucial because it provides satisfaction and pleasure, reinforcing the habit loop. It makes you feel good and ensures that your brain will remember this loop in the future, increasing the likelihood that you will repeat the behavior when the cue is encountered again. Rewards may take tangible forms, such as treats, or intangible ones, like a sense of accomplishment.

By understanding and leveraging this habit loop, you can effectively create new habits or modify existing ones. Start by carefully identifying the specific cues that trigger your current habits and the rewards that follow. Once you have a clear understanding of these elements, you can make small, manageable adjustments to the routine component of the loop. For example, if your goal is to replace a habit of snacking on unhealthy foods when stressed, you might identify stress as the cue and look for a healthier routine, such as routine, such as drinking a glass of water or going for a short walk, that offers a comparable reward. Over time, these tiny shifts in your routine will become ingrained, leading to lasting and meaningful changes in your behavior and overall lifestyle. By methodically applying this understanding of habit formation, you can achieve significant and sustainable improvements in your personal and professional life.

Why This Book?

In "Tiny Habit Shifts: Small Changes for Professional Excellence," we will delve into how you can identify your current habits, gain clarity on which habits are in line with your career goals, and implement small, manageable adjustments that can greatly improve your professional life. This book aims to be both practical and actionable, equipping you with the necessary tools and strategies to effectively implement these tiny habit shifts.

Throughout the chapters, you will discover how to pinpoint the minor changes that can yield substantial benefits. You will also learn how to navigate and overcome the various obstacles that might impede your progress. Additionally, you will find guidance on how to maintain these new habits for enduring success. Just as the British cycling team achieved phenomenal success by concentrating on marginal gains, you too can unlock extraordinary potential by leveraging the power of tiny habits.

Let's begin the journey of personal growth. We will begin by examining your existing habits and identifying those that align with your career goals. From there, we will explore the methods to make incremental changes that, over time, will lead to profound improvements in your professional life. You will be guided step-by-step through recognizing the small but impactful changes, addressing and overcoming challenges, and ensuring the longevity of your new habits.

Welcome to the start of your journey towards transformation and professional excellence. Let's embark on this path together, making one tiny shift at a time to achieve remarkable results and elevate your professional life to new heights.

Chapter 1
Setting the Foundation

"The seeds of tomorrow's achievements are

planted in today's preparations."

Identifying Your Professional Goals

Picture starting a journey without a map or a clear destination in sight. It would be chaotic, right? The same applies to your career. Mapping out your course on a map parallels the process of setting clear, actionable professional goals. It's the first, vital step towards achieving the excellence you aspire to. When you know where you're headed, every step you take becomes purposeful and meaningful.

Without a well-defined destination, it's impossible to chart a course for your career. Goals act as your guiding light, providing direction and fueling your motivation. They help you see the bigger picture and keep you focused on what truly matters. Think of goals as the benchmarks that help you measure your progress, giving you that rewarding sense of accomplishment as you tick them off one by one.

When you set specific and actionable goals, you're not just dreaming about a better future—you're creating a solid plan to make it happen. These goals are your roadmap, outlining the steps you need to take to reach your dreams. They support you in maintaining commitment, providing clarity of purpose and direction in your professional life. Each goal you achieve is a milestone, a sign that you're moving in the right direction.

By clearly defining your professional goals, you empower yourself to take charge of your career. These goals become the foundation upon which you build your strategies and actions, ensuring that every move you make is aligned with your long-term vision. They motivate you, challenge you, and provide a tangible way to measure and celebrate your achievements. So, let's embark on this journey together, setting goals that will lead you to the professional excellence you deserve.

Defining Your Goals

Let's start by painting a vivid picture of where you see yourself in the next five to ten years. Imagine the positions you dream of holding, the skills you're eager to master, and the milestones you want to reach. Take a moment to write down these visions—they're the first stepping stones on your path to success.

To manifest these dreams into reality, it's crucial to set SMART goals: Specific, Measurable, Achievable, Relevant, and Time-bound. This framework helps you turn your aspirations into practical steps you can take.

For instance, instead of setting a vague goal like "become successful," dive deeper into what success truly means to you. Think about the specifics. A SMART goal could be: "Become a project manager at a leading tech company within five years, managing projects with budgets over $1 million." This goal is specific because it outlines the exact position and responsibilities you aim for. It's measurable, with clear criteria to track your progress. It's achievable, assuming you put in the necessary effort and planning. It's relevant, aligning with your career aspirations. And it's time-bound, giving you a five-year window to reach your target.

By defining your goals this way, you give yourself a clear direction and a powerful sense of purpose. You can track your progress, celebrate your milestones, and stay motivated, knowing that each step brings you closer to your vision. So, take a deep breath, envision your future, and start setting those SMART goals that will guide you on your journey to professional excellence.

Breaking Down Your Goals

Once you've set your long-term goals, the next step is to break them down into smaller, manageable milestones. This approach transforms the journey from overwhelming to achievable, offering frequent opportunities for celebration and motivation along the way.

Take Jane, for example. Jane is a marketing executive with a dream of becoming a Chief Marketing Officer (CMO) within ten years. To make this ambitious goal more attainable, she breaks it down into smaller, actionable steps:

1. Gain proficiency in digital marketing within two years.
2. Lead a major campaign for a high-profile client within four years.
3. Obtain a marketing director position within six years.

Each of these smaller goals serves as a stepping stone towards Jane's ultimate objective. By focusing on these intermediate milestones, she can celebrate her progress regularly, stay motivated, and keep her eyes on the prize. Each accomplishment reinforces her confidence and propels her closer to her long-term vision.

Breaking down your goals in this way not only makes the overall journey less daunting but also provides clear, actionable steps that guide your daily efforts. It helps you maintain momentum, as each small victory fuels your motivation to keep pushing forward. So, identify your long-term goals and then deconstruct them into these manageable, bite-sized milestones. By doing so, you transform a lofty dream into a series of achievable steps, making your path to success clearer and more inspiring.

Creating an Action Plan

For each milestone, it's essential to develop a detailed action plan. This means identifying the skills you need to acquire, the experiences you need to gain, and the networks you need to build. Establish timelines for each action step and consistently review your progress to maintain momentum.

Let's return to Jane, our marketing executive with aspirations to become a Chief Marketing Officer (CMO). Her first milestone is gaining proficiency in digital marketing. Jane's action plan for this milestone might include:

1. Enrolling in a digital marketing certification course (6 months). This provides her with the formal education and credentials she needs.

1. Attending industry conferences and webinars (ongoing). These events keep her updated on the latest trends and allow her to network with industry professionals.

1. Taking on digital marketing projects within her current role (immediate). By applying her new knowledge in practical settings, she gains hands-on experience and demonstrates her growing expertise.

By outlining these specific actions, Jane creates a clear path forward. Each step is a building block towards her milestone, and each milestone is a step towards her ultimate goal. With this plan in place, she can track her progress, celebrate her achievements, and stay motivated.

Creating an action plan transforms your goals from abstract ideas into concrete steps. It provides a clear road-map that guides your efforts and keeps you focused on what needs to be done. Regularly reviewing your action plan ensures that you remain aligned with your goals and can make adjustments as needed. So, take each milestone and break it down into actionable steps. Define what skills, experiences, and connections you need, set your time-lines, and commit to regular progress reviews. This way, you keep your journey to professional excellence structured, achievable, and inspiring.

Assessing Your Current Habits

To initiate meaningful changes in your life, it's essential to first understand your existing habits. This begins with conducting a thorough assessment of your daily routines, identifying which habits align with your goals and which ones act as obstacles.

Conducting a Habit Inventory

Begin by recording your daily activities throughout the week. Pay close attention to both your professional tasks and personal routines. Document the time allocated to each activity and take note of your emotions during and after each task.

Consider John, a software engineer, as an example. John decides to keep a detailed log and discovers several insights about his habits:

A. He spends two hours every evening watching TV, which leaves him feeling lethargic.
B. He experiences a slump in energy levels after lunch, affecting his productivity.
C. He tends to procrastinate on starting his coding tasks until late in the day, which delays his progress.

This habit inventory provides John with valuable insights into both his productive and unproductive behaviors. By identifying these patterns, he can begin to make informed decisions about which habits to maintain, modify, or eliminate altogether.

By conducting a habit inventory, you gain a deeper understanding of how your daily routines impact your overall effectiveness and well-being. This awareness serves as the foundation for making strategic adjustments that align with your goals and enhance your productivity. So, take the time to assess your current habits thoroughly. Document your activities, reflect on their outcomes, and use these insights to pave the way for positive change in your professional and personal life.

Identifying Productive and Unproductive Habits

Once you've compiled your activity log, it's time to analyze it for patterns. Look closely at which activities support your goals and which ones detract from them, considering both their impact on your productivity and energy levels.

For instance, John reviews his log and makes several observations:

His two-hour nightly TV habit doesn't contribute to his goal of mastering a new programming language. Instead, it leaves him feeling lethargic and unproductive.

On the other hand, John recognizes that his morning routine of reading tech blogs keeps him informed about industry trends. This habit aligns with his goal of staying updated and enhances his professional knowledge.

By identifying these patterns, John gains clarity on which habits are productive and which are not. This awareness enables him to prioritize activities that contribute to his professional growth while considering adjustments to reduce or eliminate habits that hinder his progress.

Analyzing your habits in this way allows you to make informed decisions about where to focus your time and energy. It empowers you to cultivate habits that support your goals and discard those that hold you back. So, take the time to reflect on your activity log, recognize the impact of each habit, and make conscious choices to optimize your daily routines for success and fulfillment.

Evaluating Habit Impact

To effectively evaluate the impact of your habits, consider their influence on both your productivity and overall well-being. Ask yourself critical questions to assess each habit:

•1. Does this habit move me closer to my professional goals? Evaluate whether the habit contributes directly to your career aspirations or detracts from them.

•2. How does this habit make me feel—energized, drained, focused, distracted? Consider and evaluate the emotional and physical impacts of each habit. Consider whether it boosts your energy and focus or leaves you feeling depleted and distracted.

•3. Is there a more effective way to organize my time? Explore alternative ways to allocate your time that could enhance your productivity and align more closely with your goals.

For example, John conducts a self-assessment and realizes that his nightly TV routine doesn't align with his goal of mastering a new programming language. It consumes valuable time and leaves him feeling lethargic rather than energized.

In contrast, he acknowledges that coding practice sessions energize him and directly contribute to his professional growth.

Consequently, John decides to replace his evening TV habit with a coding practice session. This adjustment not only aligns his daily routine more closely with his career goals but also enhances his productivity and sense of fulfillment.

By evaluating the impact of each habit through these lenses, you can make informed decisions about which behaviors to maintain, modify, or discard. This self-awareness empowers you to cultivate habits that support your professional ambitions and enhance your overall well-being. So, take the time to assess your habits thoughtfully, considering their effects on your goals and daily life. Make adjustments as needed to optimize your routines for success and personal satisfaction.

The Science Behind Habit Formation

Understanding the mechanisms of habit formation and change is essential for making effective adjustments to your behaviors. Habits are automatic responses triggered by specific cues and reinforced by rewards.

The Habit Loop

The habit loop comprises three key components:

Cue : This is the signal that kickstarts the habit. It could be a particular time of day, an emotional state like stress or boredom, or a specific event in your environment.

Routine : The routine is the actual behavior or action you engage in once the cue is encountered. It's the habitual response you perform almost automatically.

Reward : After completing the routine, you receive a reward - a positive reinforcement. This might bring a sense of pleasure, relief, or satisfaction. The reward reinforces the habit loop, making it more likely that you'll repeat the behavior in similar situations in the future.

For Example, Consider Mary, a sales executive. During her work breaks, Mary habitually checks social media. Here's how the habit loop applies to her:

•Cue: Mary feels bored or fatigued during her work break.

•Routine: She scrolls through her social media feeds to alleviate boredom.

•Reward: Mary experiences brief entertainment or distraction, which provides a temporary mental break.

By recognizing the components of her habit loop—cue, routine, and reward—Mary gains insight into why she engages in this behavior. Understanding this process empowers her to make conscious choices about whether to maintain, modify, or replace this habit with a more productive or fulfilling alternative.

Understanding the science behind habit formation enables you to identify patterns in your own behavior and take intentional steps to cultivate new, beneficial habits. By adjusting the cues and rewards associated with your routines, you can effectively reshape your habits and enhance your personal and professional life.

Changing Habits with Tiny Shifts

When you aim to change a habit, begin by identifying the cue that triggers it and the reward it provides. Then, replace the routine with a new behavior that offers a similar reward.

For instance, Mary recognizes that her habit of checking social media during breaks is a distraction. She identifies the cue (feeling bored) and the reward (brief entertainment). To foster a more productive habit, Mary decides to substitute her routine with a quick walk or a short reading break instead. These activities provide a similar reward of mental refreshment but better align with her goal of maintaining focus and productivity.

By making these small adjustments, Mary transforms her habit loop. She retains the positive reward she seeks while steering her behavior towards activities that support her professional objectives. This approach illustrates the power of tiny shifts in habit formation, demonstrating how deliberate changes can lead to significant improvements in personal effectiveness and well-being.

Building New Habits

Establishing new habits follows a similar loop to changing existing ones. Select a straightforward and specific behavior you wish to cultivate into a habit, identify a cue to prompt its initiation, and determine a reward to reinforce its continuity.

For example, suppose you aspire to develop a habit of networking regularly. You might set a goal to connect with one new professional contact each week. In this scenario:

Cue: Use your weekly review meeting as a cue to prompt networking efforts.

Routine: Reach out to a new contact, initiate a conversation, or attend a networking event.

Reward: Enjoy the satisfaction of expanding your professional network, gaining new insights, or establishing potential collaborations.

By adhering to this structured approach, you transform networking into a consistent habit. This method underscores the effectiveness of small, deliberate actions in fostering long-term professional growth and success.

Consistency and Reinforcement

Building habits relies on repetition and consistency. Start with small steps to ensure you can sustain the new behavior over time. Celebrate even minor successes to reinforce the habit.

Consider Jane, our aspiring Chief Marketing Officer (CMO), who aims to stay updated on industry trends. She sets a goal to read one article on marketing innovations each morning:

Cue: Her morning coffee serves as a prompt to begin her day with new insights.

Routine: Jane reads the selected article, absorbing valuable information.

Reward: She gains knowledge that keeps her current in her field and feels a sense of accomplishment toward her career goals.

By applying the principles of the habit loop—cue, routine, reward—Jane systematically integrates this practice into her daily routine. This approach not only helps her stay informed but also reinforces her commitment to professional growth.

Understanding and harnessing the habit loop empowers you to systematically build new habits and replace old ones. This method establishes a robust foundation for achieving your professional aspirations, one consistent step at a time.

What We Discovered

Setting the foundation for professional excellence requires a comprehensive approach that integrates understanding your goals, assessing your habits, and strategically forming new behaviors. By breaking down your long-term objectives into manageable steps, evaluating your daily routines, and leveraging the science of habit formation, you can enact small yet impactful changes that pave the way for substantial and sustainable progress in your career.

By aligning your actions with your aspirations, you cultivate a path towards achieving professional excellence. Each deliberate step forward, informed by clear goals and supported by effective habits, propels you closer to realizing your full potential in your chosen field.

Embrace this journey of continuous improvement, where each adjustment and achievement builds upon the last. With dedication and persistence, you can cultivate a professional life defined by growth, fulfillment, and success.

With this foundation in place, you're well on your way to achieving professional excellence through tiny habit shifts. Let's dive deeper into the specifics of building effective routines in the next chapter.

With this foundation in place, you're well on your way to achieving professional excellence through tiny habit shifts. Let's dive deeper into the specifics of building effective routines in the next chapter.

Here's a table listing the top 5 positive and top 5 negative habits of professionals, including the cue, routine, and reward for each habit.

SR. No.	Positive Habits	Cue	Routine	Reward
1.	Morning Planning	Start of the workday	Creating a daily to-do list	Clear direction and productivity
2.	Regular Exercise	Scheduled time (e.g., morning)	Exercising (jogging, gym, etc.)	Improved energy and health
3.	Continuous Learning	Free time or lunch break	Reading industry-related articles/books	Knowledge gain and skill enhancement
4.	Networking	End of a project or event	Reaching out to new contacts on LinkedIn	Expanded professional network
5.	Time Blocking	Beginning of the workweek	Scheduling tasks in blocks	Increased focus and efficiency

SR. No.	Negative Habits	Cue	Routine	Reward
1.	Procrastination	Feeling overwhelmed or bored	Delaying important tasks	Temporary relief from stress
2.	Multitasking	Seeing multiple tasks at once	Trying to work on several tasks simultaneously	Perceived increase in productivity
3.	Excessive Social Media Use	Feeling bored or during breaks	Scrolling through social media feeds	Short-term entertainment
4.	Skipping Breaks	Tight deadlines or heavy workload	Working through breaks	Perceived increase in productivity
5.	Poor Sleep Hygiene	Late-night work or screen time	Staying up late	Temporary sense of productivity or relaxation

By identifying and understanding these habits along with their cues, routines, and rewards, professionals can work towards reinforcing positive habits and replacing negative ones with more productive behaviors.

Did you know?

Contrary to the popular belief in a "21-day rule" for habit formation, studies indicate that forming a new habit can take significantly longer. On average, it takes about 21 days to start forming a new habit, but this time-frame can vary widely among individuals. In reality, habit formation can take anywhere from 18 to 254 days, depending on factors such as the complexity of the behavior and individual differences in motivation and consistency.

Understanding this variability underscores the importance of patience and persistence when cultivating new habits. It highlights the need to focus on consistent effort and gradual progress rather than expecting immediate results.

By embracing this understanding, you can approach habit formation with realistic expectations and adapt your strategies accordingly to achieve lasting change.

19

Chapter 2
Recognizing Your Existing Habits

"Self-awareness is the foundation of habit change;

see clearly to change profoundly."

Understanding and recognizing your existing habits is a vital step toward making meaningful changes in your professional life. This chapter will guide you through the process of mapping your daily routines, identifying both positive and negative habits, and understanding the triggers that drive these behaviors. By the end of this chapter, you'll have a comprehensive picture of your current habits and be better prepared to make the necessary adjustments for achieving professional excellence.

Mapping your daily routines involves taking a detailed inventory of your activities, noting how you spend your time and the outcomes of these actions. Identifying positive habits helps you understand what is working well, while recognizing negative habits highlights areas needing improvement. Understanding habit triggers—those cues that initiate certain behaviors—provides insights into why you act the way you do.

Armed with this knowledge, you can start making informed decisions about which habits to maintain, modify, or eliminate, setting the stage for a more focused and productive professional journey.

Mapping Your Daily Routines

The first step in recognizing your existing habits is to map out your daily routines. This involves tracking your activities and behaviors throughout the day to see where your time goes and identify patterns. By gaining a clear picture of your daily habits, you can make informed decisions about which behaviors to maintain, adjust, or replace.

Step-by-Step Guide to Mapping Your Daily Routines

1. Start with a Log: Begin by keeping a detailed log of your daily activities for at least a week. Note down everything you do from the moment you wake up until you go to bed. Include both work-related tasks and personal activities. This comprehensive approach ensures you capture all aspects of your routine.

2. Record Time and Duration: For each activity, record the start time and the duration. This helps you see how much time you spend on different tasks and activities, providing a clearer picture of your daily time allocation.

3. Include Context: Note the context or situation in which each activity takes place. For example, record whether you were at your desk, in a meeting, or commuting. Also, note any emotions or thoughts you experienced during these activities. Understanding the context and your emotional state can provide valuable insights into why certain habits exist.

4. Review and Analyze: At the end of the week, review your log. Look for patterns and regular routines. Identify which activities are habitual and which are sporadic. Analyze how these routines align with your professional goals and overall well-being.

By following this step-by-step guide, you can systematically map your daily routines and gain a deeper understanding of your habits. This awareness is the foundation for making effective changes, allowing you to optimize your daily activities and create a path toward professional excellence.

John's log reveals several habitual activities, such as checking his phone first thing in the morning and taking a coffee break at 11:30 AM. By mapping his routine, John can now analyze these habits and their impact on his productivity and well-being.

Identifying Positive and Negative Habits

With a clear map of your daily routines, the next step is to identify which habits are beneficial (positive) and which are detrimental (negative) to your professional goals.

Evaluating Your Habits

1. Positive Habits: These are behaviors that contribute to your productivity, health, and overall professional growth. Positive habits are aligned with your goals and enhance your performance.

Examples of Positive Habits:

- Starting your day by outlining tasks on a checklist (by making a to-do list)

- Incorporating regular breaks to sustain focus

- Engaging in continuous learning or skill development

- Networking with peers and mentors

Recognizing these positive habits allows you to reinforce them, ensuring they remain a consistent part of your routine.

2. Negative Habits: These are behaviors that hinder your progress, drain your energy, or waste your time. Negative habits distract you from your goals and reduce your efficiency.

Examples of Negative Habits:

- Procrastinating on important tasks

- Devoting an inordinate amount of time to social networking platforms.

- Missing meals or working late into the night

- Avoiding difficult conversations or feedback

Identifying these negative habits is the first step toward addressing and replacing them with more productive behaviors.

By evaluating your habits through this lens, you can clearly see which behaviors to cultivate and which to change. This understanding sets the stage for making strategic adjustments to your daily routines, ultimately guiding you toward professional excellence.

Example: John's Habit Analysis

Based on his daily log, John identifies the following positive and negative habits:

Positive Habits	Cue	Routine	Reward
Morning workout	Waking up	Exercising in home gym	Increased energy and alertness
Focused coding sessions	Start of work	Coding for 2 hours without interruption	High productivity and progress
Evening walk	End of workday	Walking in the neighborhood	Relaxation and mental clarity

Negative Habits	Cue	Routine	Reward
Checking phone first thing in the morning	Waking up	Browsing emails and social media	Temporary engagement but grogginess
Social media during coffee break	Feeling distracted	Scrolling through social media	Short-term entertainment but distraction
Watching TV for 2 hours in the evening	Leisure time after dinner	Watching TV	Relaxation but potential overindulgence

John's log reveals several habitual activities, such as checking his phone first thing in the morning and taking a coffee break at 11:30 AM. By mapping his routine, John can now analyze these habits and their impact on his productivity and well-being.

Understanding Habit Triggers

To effectively change your habits, you need to understand the triggers that initiate them. A habit trigger, or cue, is the event or circumstance that prompts habitual behavior. Recognizing and comprehending these triggers allows you to strategically adjust your routines and cultivate new, beneficial habits.

Types of Habit Triggers

1. Time-Based Triggers : Certain times of the day can trigger specific habits. For example, you might have a habit of drinking coffee every morning at 10 AM. Recognizing time-based triggers helps you anticipate and prepare for habitual actions, making it easier to modify or replace them.

2. Event-Based Triggers : Specific events or actions can act as triggers. For instance, finishing a meeting might trigger the habit of checking your phone. By identifying these event-based triggers, you can plan alternative actions that align better with your professional goals.

3. Emotional Triggers : Emotions can also serve as triggers. For example, feeling stressed might trigger the habit of eating comfort food. Understanding emotional triggers allows you to develop healthier coping mechanisms and replace unproductive habits with more beneficial ones.

4. Environmental Triggers : Your surroundings can trigger habits. For instance, walking into your office might trigger the habit of checking your email. Being aware of environmental triggers helps you create a workspace that supports positive habits and minimizes distractions.

By comprehensively understanding the various types of habit triggers, you can gain better control over your behaviors. This awareness empowers you to make deliberate changes to your routines, fostering habits that contribute to your professional excellence and personal well-being.

Example: Identifying John's Habit Triggers

John analyzes the triggers for his positive and negative habits:

Habit	Trigger (Cue)
Morning workout	Waking up
Focused coding sessions	Starting work
Evening walk	Ending the workday
Checking phone in the morning	Waking up
Social media during coffee break	Feeling distracted or bored
Watching TV in the evening	Post-dinner leisure time

By identifying these triggers, John gains insight into the cues that drive his habits. This knowledge empowers him to make strategic changes to his routines when specific cues occur.

For example, John realizes that waking up triggers both his morning workout and the habit of checking his phone. To foster a more positive start to his day, he decides to replace checking his phone with a quick stretch or drinking a glass of water. This small shift helps set a positive tone for the day, reinforcing a healthier and more productive morning routine.

Understanding and addressing these triggers enables John to systematically replace unproductive habits with beneficial ones, aligning his daily behaviors with his long-term professional goals and personal well-being.

What We Discovered ?

Recognizing your existing habits involves mapping your daily routines, identifying which habits are positive or negative, and understanding the triggers that initiate these habits. This awareness is the foundation for making intentional changes that will lead to professional excellence. By systematically analyzing and adjusting your habits, you can create a more productive, focused, and fulfilling professional life.

In the next chapter, we will explore how to set and achieve small, actionable goals that align with your professional aspirations, building on the foundation we've established here. Through this process, you'll learn how to break down your long-term objectives into manageable steps, ensuring steady progress toward your ultimate career goals. Prepare to take the next step in your journey to professional excellence, equipped with the knowledge and strategies to transform your habits and achieve lasting success.

Did you know?

Up to 40% of our daily actions are habitual, meaning they are performed automatically without conscious thought. This significant portion of our daily behavior underscores the power and influence of habits in our lives. Recognizing and understanding these existing habits is the first step toward making positive changes in your life and achieving your goals. By becoming aware of the routines that shape your day, you can intentionally modify them to better align with your aspirations, paving the way for personal and professional growth.

Chapter 3
Aligning Habits with Professional Goals

"Professional excellence is achieved by

cultivating habits that support your aspirations."

By consciously aligning your habits with your goals, you are setting yourself up for success in a powerful way. Each small action you take becomes a stepping stone towards achieving your bigger vision, creating a sense of momentum and progress that is both motivating and rewarding.

In this chapter, we will explore the importance of defining key habits that will support your professional journey. By identifying the habits that are most closely linked to your goals, you can prioritize them and focus your energy on cultivating those behaviors that will have the greatest impact on your success.

We will also discuss how to create a habit-goal alignment plan that ensures you are consistently moving in the right direction. By establishing daily routines and rituals that reinforce your desired habits, you can build a solid foundation for long-term growth and achievement.

Ultimately, by aligning your habits with your goals and taking intentional action each day, you can unlock new levels of potential and reach heights that once seemed out of reach. As you work towards aligning your habits with your goals, it's important to stay committed and disciplined in your daily actions. Consistency is key to creating lasting change and progress. By staying focused on your habit-goal alignment plan, you can overcome obstacles and setbacks that may arise along the way. This chapter will guide you through the process of harnessing the power of consistency and discipline to achieve your desired outcomes. Remember, persistent small daily actions compound over time to produce substantial outcomes. Stay dedicated to your habits and goals, and you will see the positive impact they have on your life. Embrace the path of growth and transformation as you strive to achieve your fullest potential.

Defining Key Habits for Success

By identifying and adopting these key habits for success, you can start to emulate the behaviors and mindset of those who have achieved greatness. Whether it's setting specific goals, practicing discipline, networking effectively, or constantly seeking self-improvement, these habits can help you navigate the challenges and opportunities that come your way in your career. It's not just about what you do occasionally, but rather the consistent actions you take every day that will ultimately determine your success. So let's commit to developing and maintaining these habits, knowing that they will be the foundation for our own journey towards achieving our career goals.

Finding Your Key Habits

Successful professionals often leave behind a trail of habits that paved their way to success. To uncover these gems, immerse yourself in their stories. Dive deep into biographies, interviews, and articles that recount their journeys. Pay attention not just to their achievements, but to the daily rituals and behaviors that propelled them forward. What patterns emerge? Perhaps you'll discover a commitment to early morning routines, a dedication to continuous learning, or a consistent practice of reflection. These habits, when dissected, reveal actionable insights that you can adapt to your own journey.

Research and Learn: Dive into the lives of successful professionals in your field.

To truly understand the essence of success, immerse yourself in the narratives of those who have achieved greatness. Take the time to read biographies that detail their triumphs and setbacks, watch interviews where they candidly share their experiences, and absorb articles that analyze their strategies. It's not just about gathering facts; it's about uncovering the underlying habits and mindsets that set them apart. For instance, you might find that many successful individuals maintain a disciplined morning routine that kickstarts their day with clarity and purpose. Others may stress the significance of lifelong learning, continually pursuing new knowledge and skills to maintain a competitive edge in their field.

Absorb the habits that have driven their success. What patterns do you see?

As you delve into their stories, pay close attention to the recurring patterns of behavior that underpin their achievements. These patterns are often the key to unlocking their success formula. Perhaps you notice a consistent commitment to setting and achieving goals, or a habit of networking and building meaningful relationships within their industry. These observations not only reveal the external actions but also shed light on their internal mindset and beliefs. By identifying these patterns, you can start to discern which habits align with your own values and aspirations.

Understand their journeys and adapt actionable insights to your own path.

It's crucial to go beyond surface-level success stories and understand the journeys that led these professionals to where they are today. By dissecting their habits and rituals, you can extract actionable insights that resonate with your own ambitions. For example, if resilience in the face of adversity emerges as a common trait among successful individuals, you can cultivate practices that strengthen your own resilience. By adapting these insights to suit your unique circumstances, you pave the way for personal growth and achievement in your chosen field.

Let's elaborate on Anna's journey of discovering key habits:

Meet Anna, a driven marketing manager with aspirations of climbing the corporate ladder to become a marketing director. In her quest for success, Anna closely observes the habits of the accomplished directors within her company. What does she notice?

Stay Updated : Anna discovers that successful directors make it a priority to stay informed about industry trends and developments. They avidly read industry reports, research articles, and subscribe to newsletters that keep them abreast of the latest innovations and insights. By staying updated, they not only enhance their knowledge but also position themselves as thought leaders in their field.

Network Effectively : Networking isn't just a social activity for these directors; it's a strategic endeavor. They actively cultivate and nurture relationships with key stakeholders, industry peers, and potential collaborators. Through effective networking, they not only expand their professional circle but also gain valuable perspectives and opportunities that propel their careers forward.

Analyze Data : Data analysis is central to their approach, guiding their decision-making process. Anna notices that successful directors rely heavily on data analytics to inform their strategic decisions. They meticulously analyze market trends, consumer behavior patterns, and performance metrics to identify opportunities and optimize outcomes. By leveraging data effectively, they minimize risks and maximize returns for their projects and initiatives.

Innovate : Creativity and innovation are integral to their success. Anna observes that these directors carve out dedicated time for brainstorming sessions and creative thinking exercises. They promote an innovative culture within their teams, creating an environment that embraces new ideas and encourages experimentation. By prioritizing innovation, they stay ahead of competitors and drive continuous growth and improvement within their organization.

Manage Time : Time management is another key habit that sets them apart. Anna notices that successful directors are masters of their schedules. They meticulously plan their days, setting clear priorities and allocating time effectively to critical tasks and projects. This disciplined approach not only boosts productivity but also ensures that they consistently deliver results in a timely manner.

Armed with these insights, Anna sees a clear path forward in her own career journey. By integrating these key habits into her daily routine—whether it's dedicating time for industry research, nurturing professional relationships, embracing data-driven insights, fostering creativity, or optimizing her time management skills—Anna is poised to accelerate her career growth and achieve her goal of becoming a marketing director.

Prioritizing Habits That Matter

In the pursuit of personal and professional growth, not all habits are created equal. Some habits have a profound impact on your success trajectory, while others may not contribute as significantly. The key to accelerating your progress lies in identifying and prioritizing the habits that yield the greatest results.

Consider this: successful individuals don't just adopt random habits—they strategically focus their energy on activities that align with their goals and aspirations. It's about making conscious choices and channeling your efforts where they can make the most significant difference.

For example, imagine a successful entrepreneur who attributes much of their success to their morning routine. By starting each day with meditation and goal-setting, they cultivate a mindset of clarity and purpose that permeates their decision-making throughout the day. This deliberate habit sets the tone for productivity and resilience in the face of challenges.

Moreover, prioritizing habits involves understanding the ripple effects they create in your life. A habit like regular exercise not only improves physical health but also enhances mental clarity and boosts energy levels, thereby increasing overall productivity and resilience.

Ultimately, prioritizing habits that matter is about intentional living. It's about identifying the behaviors that align with your values, goals, and vision for the future. By focusing your energy on cultivating these habits, you create a powerful foundation for continuous growth and achievement.

Evaluating Habit Impact

When it comes to cultivating habits that lead to success, evaluating their impact is crucial. Consider these three crucial factors :

1. Relevance to Goals : How closely does this habit align with your professional goals?

The first step in evaluating a habit's impact is to assess its alignment with your overarching objectives. Ask yourself: Does this habit contribute directly to my professional aspirations? For instance, if your goal is to enhance leadership skills, cultivating a habit of regular feedback sessions with your team can significantly align with this objective. By ensuring that each habit is purposefully chosen to support your long-term goals, you create a strategic framework for growth and achievement.

2. Effectiveness : Does this habit significantly enhance your performance and results?

Effectiveness is about measuring the tangible benefits that a habit brings to your professional life. Consider how this habit influences your productivity, decision-making, or overall performance metrics. For example, if you adopt a habit of daily reflection and goal-setting, observe how it improves your clarity of thought and ability to prioritize tasks effectively. By tracking the outcomes associated with each habit, you can gauge its effectiveness in driving measurable results.

3. Feasibility : How practical is it to incorporate this habit into your daily routine?

Feasibility is a critical factor in sustaining habits over the long term. Evaluate whether the habit is realistic within the context of your current schedule, resources, and lifestyle. A habit that requires minimal time investment or can be integrated seamlessly into your existing routines is more likely to be sustainable. Conversely, overly ambitious habits that demand excessive effort or disrupt your daily flow may be harder to maintain. Choose habits that are practical and align with your lifestyle to ensure consistent adherence and long-term success.

By systematically evaluating habits based on their relevance to goals, effectiveness in enhancing performance, and feasibility in daily practice, you empower yourself to make informed choices that accelerate your professional growth and success.

Let's see how Anna Prioritized Habits for herself :

TINY HABIT SHIFTS

As Anna charts her path to becoming a marketing director, she carefully evaluates the impact of her key habits:

Staying Updated : Anna recognizes the importance of staying abreast of industry trends and insights. By dedicating time each day to reading industry reports and relevant articles, she ensures that her decisions are informed and aligned with current market dynamics. This habit not only enhances her knowledge but also positions her as a proactive and insightful leader within her field.

Networking : Networking plays a pivotal role in Anna's career advancement strategy. She commits to attending weekly networking events and actively engages with industry professionals on LinkedIn daily. By cultivating meaningful relationships and expanding her professional network, Anna opens doors to new opportunities, mentorship, and collaborative ventures that propel her career forward.

Data Analysis : Anna understands the power of data-driven decision-making. Twice a week, she sets aside dedicated sessions to analyze market trends, consumer behavior data, and performance metrics. This disciplined approach enables her to derive actionable insights that inform strategic initiatives and optimize outcomes for her projects.

Innovating : Innovation fuels Anna's leadership in creative projects. She carves out regular time for brainstorming sessions and creative thinking exercises, fostering a culture of innovation within her team. By encouraging fresh ideas and novel approaches, Anna drives continuous improvement and distinguishes herself as a forward-thinking leader in her organization.

Time Management : Recognizing the value of productivity, Anna adopts effective time management practices. Utilizing planning tools and maintaining a consistent daily routine, she prioritizes tasks strategically and allocates time efficiently. This habit not only enhances her productivity but also ensures that she meets deadlines consistently and delivers results with precision.

By prioritizing these high-impact habits—staying updated, networking effectively, leveraging data analysis, fostering innovation, and mastering time management—Anna not only enhances her professional capabilities but also positions herself for significant career advancement and success as a marketing director.

Creating a Habit - Goal Alignment Plan

Now that you've identified and prioritized your key habits, it's time to create a plan that seamlessly integrates these habits into your daily routine, ensuring they are aligned with your professional goals.

Crafting this Habit-Goal Alignment Plan starts with defining your career objectives clearly. Whether your aim is to rise to a leadership role, master a new skill, or boost productivity, clarity on your goals sets the stage for selecting and aligning habits effectively.

Align each habit with specific milestones or outcomes you aim to achieve. For instance, if leadership development is your goal, focus on habits like networking strategically, seeking mentorship, and engaging in regular feedback sessions. These actions directly contribute to enhancing your leadership capabilities over time.

Integrate your chosen habits into your daily routine in a practical and sustainable manner. Consider your peak performance hours and existing commitments when scheduling activities like data analysis or skill-building exercises. By slotting these tasks into your day effectively, you ensure they become consistent practices rather than occasional endeavors.

Establishing accountability mechanisms is crucial. Whether through journaling progress, using habit-tracking tools, or partnering with a mentor, accountability keeps you focused on adhering to your plan. Regularly reviewing your performance allows for adjustments that keep you on track towards achieving your career goals.

By aligning your key habits with your professional aspirations in a structured Habit-Goal Alignment Plan, you pave the way for continuous growth and success in your career journey.

Step-by-Step Guide to Your Habit-Goal Alignment Plan

Creating a Habit-Goal Alignment Plan is a structured approach to integrating your key habits with your professional goals. Here's a step-by-step guide to help you implement this plan effectively:

1. Define Clear Goals: Start with clarity :

Begin by defining your professional goals using the SMART framework—Specific, Measurable, Achievable, Relevant, and Time-bound. This approach ensures that your goals are well-defined and actionable. For example, instead of setting a vague goal like "improve leadership skills," you might specify "achieve certification in leadership training within six months."

1. **List Your Key Habits :**

Write down the habits you've identified and prioritized.

Make a list of the habits that align with your defined goals. These could include habits such as daily networking activities, weekly skill-building exercises, or monthly progress assessments. Each habit should directly contribute to moving you closer to your desired outcomes.

1. **Schedule Your Habits:**

Find a place for each habit in your daily or weekly schedule. Integrate your identified habits into your routine in a practical and sustainable way. Consider your daily rhythm and commitments when scheduling activities like data analysis or professional development sessions. Consistency in practicing these habits is crucial for sustained long-term success.

1. **Monitor Your Progress :**

Utilize a habit tracker to keep tabs on your development.

Implement a habit-tracking system—whether it's through a journal, a mobile app, or a simple checklist—to monitor your adherence to each habit. Tracking your progress allows you to stay accountable and provides insights into areas where you may need to adjust your approach.

1. **Review and Adjust :**

Regularly review your progress and be open to adjustments. Set aside time to review your performance against your goals and habits. If you find that certain habits are not yielding the expected results or are challenging to maintain, be proactive in tweaking your approach. Flexibility and willingness to adapt ensure that your Habit-Goal Alignment Plan remains effective and aligned with your evolving professional journey.

By following this step-by-step guide, you create a structured framework that integrates purposeful habits with your career aspirations, paving the way for continuous growth and achievement.

Have a look at Anna's Habit-Goal Alignment Plan.

Her Goal: Become a Marketing Director within three years.

Anna's path to achieving her goal of becoming a Marketing Director is guided by a strategic Habit-Goal Alignment Plan. Here's how she integrates key habits into her daily routine:

1. Staying Updated :

Routine : Anna starts each morning with 30 minutes of reading industry articles and books.

Cue : Her morning coffee serves as a signal to begin her reading routine.

Reward : Anna feels informed and ahead of industry trends, reinforcing her confidence and expertise.

2. Networking :

Routine : Anna attends one networking event per week and connects with one new professional on LinkedIn daily.

Cue : A weekly calendar reminder prompts her to plan and attend networking events.

Reward : Through expanded professional connections, Anna discovers new opportunities and strengthens her industry influence.

3. Data Analysis :

Routine : Anna dedicates one hour every Tuesday and Thursday afternoon to analyzing marketing data.

Cue : Post-lunch is her scheduled time for deep dives into data analysis.

Reward : By gaining actionable insights, Anna enhances her decision-making abilities and improves campaign strategies.

4. Innovating :

Routine: Anna sets aside one hour every Wednesday morning for dedicated brainstorming sessions.

Cue : A mid-week reminder prompts her to engage in creative thinking.

Reward : These sessions spark innovative ideas and pave the way for groundbreaking marketing campaigns.

5. Time Management :

Routine : Anna begins each day by planning her tasks and reviews her accomplishments each evening.

Cue : Her daily work routine starts and ends with these planning sessions.

Reward : This disciplined approach enhances Anna's productivity, providing clarity and focus throughout her workday.

Tracking and Reviewing

To ensure she stays on track with her Habit-Goal Alignment Plan, Anna incorporates robust tracking and review mechanisms into her routine:

Habit Tracking App : Anna utilizes a habit tracking app to log her daily and weekly activities. This allows her to monitor her adherence to each habit and track her progress over time. By maintaining a digital record of her habits, Anna stays accountable and gains valuable insights into her consistency and areas for improvement.

Monthly Review : Anna schedules a monthly review session to assess her overall progress and make necessary adjustments to her habits. During this review, she reflects on her achievements, evaluates any challenges encountered, and identifies opportunities for refinement. By conducting regular reviews, Anna ensures that her Habit-Goal Alignment Plan remains aligned with her career goals and adaptable to changing circumstances.

By meticulously scheduling and adhering to these key habits—staying updated, networking effectively, analyzing data rigorously, fostering innovation, and managing time efficiently—Anna is positioning herself for steady progress towards her career aspirations as a Marketing Director.

What We Discovered ?

Aligning your habits with your professional goals is a potent strategy for achieving success. By identifying key habits, prioritizing those that have the greatest impact, and crafting a habit-goal alignment plan, you can ensure that each day propels you closer to your career aspirations. This method transforms your daily actions into a dynamic catalyst for professional growth, harnessing the profound influence of incremental habit shifts.

In the next chapter, we will explore how to build and sustain new habits, providing practical strategies to ensure your new habits become ingrained and lead to lasting change. Together, we'll continue this journey toward professional excellence, one habit at a time.

Below is a sample data sheet designed to help a sales executive align their habits with their professional goals. This sheet can be customized to fit individual needs and preferences.

39

Habit	Cue	Routine	Reward	Frequency
Prospecting	Start of the workday	Spend 1 hour identifying and contacting new leads	Increased pipeline of potential clients	Daily (Monday-Friday)
Follow-Up	End of the workday	Spend 30 minutes sending follow-up emails or calls	Strengthened client relationships	Daily (Monday-Friday)
Learning & Development	Lunch break	Read sales books, articles, or attend webinars for 30 minutes	Enhanced sales skills and knowledge	Daily
Networking	Weekly team meeting	Connect with one new professional on LinkedIn or attend events	Expanded professional network	Weekly
Reviewing Performance	End of the week	Analyze weekly sales performance and set goals for next week	Insights gained for continuous improvement	Weekly
Time Management	Start of the workday	Plan daily tasks and prioritize activities	Increased productivity and efficiency	Daily
Customer Relationship Management	Post-lunch	Update CRM with new information and track progress	Organized client data and better follow-up	Daily (Monday-Friday)
Pitch Practice	After team meetings	Practice sales pitches with a colleague	Improved sales presentations	Weekly
Product Knowledge	Morning coffee	Spend 15 minutes reviewing product features and benefits	Better product understanding	Daily
Stress Management	Mid-afternoon break	Take a 10-minute meditation or walk	Reduced stress and increased focus	Daily

As per this sample sheet, you can create a sheet suitable to your profession and goals.

Did you know?

According to a study by psychologist Gail Matthews, people are 42% more likely to achieve their goals when they write them down. This highlights the importance of defining clear, actionable habits that align with your professional objectives. By committing your goals to writing and breaking them down into specific habits, you increase your chances of success and pave the way for professional excellence.

Chapter 4:
Making Tiny Habit Shifts

"Small changes in habits can spark major progress,

with each step helping you reach your ultimate target."

In the journey toward achieving professional excellence, the most impactful changes often stem from small, consistent adjustments. This chapter dives deep into the principle of making tiny habit shifts. It offers practical strategies to facilitate these gradual improvements and showcases real-life examples illustrating how even minor changes can lead to significant professional growth.

By focusing on making tiny habit shifts, you empower yourself to cultivate habits that support your long-term goals. These shifts aren't about drastic overhauls but rather about making manageable adjustments in your daily routine. For instance, allocating just ten minutes each morning to review industry news or dedicating a brief period each day for skill development can accumulate into substantial advancements over time. Such deliberate actions not only enhance your skills but also foster a mindset of continuous improvement.

Real-life examples vividly demonstrate the power of tiny habit shifts. Professionals who consistently allocate time for self-reflection or adopt a habit of seeking feedback regularly often find themselves better equipped to navigate challenges and seize opportunities. These incremental changes build resilience, adaptability, and a proactive approach to professional development.

In essence, making tiny habit shifts is about embracing the journey of improvement and growth. It's about recognizing that lasting progress often arises from consistent, small actions rather than occasional bursts of effort. By integrating these strategies into your routine, you lay a robust foundation for achieving sustained success and realizing your professional aspirations.

The Principle of Small Changes

The concept of making tiny habit shifts is rooted in the understanding that small, manageable changes are easier to maintain and can lead to lasting transformation. Rather than aiming for drastic overhauls, which can be overwhelming and unsustainable, focus on incremental improvements that accumulate over time. This approach leverages the power of gradual, steady progress, making it a practical and effective strategy for personal and professional growth.

When you concentrate on making small changes, you avoid the pitfalls of trying to implement radical transformations that are difficult to sustain. These minor adjustments can seamlessly integrate into your daily routine without causing significant disruption. Over time, these small changes can collectively bring about substantial improvements, leading to lasting and meaningful transformation.

By prioritizing incremental improvements, you create a sustainable path to achieving your goals. This method not only reduces the stress and resistance associated with major changes but also fosters a sense of accomplishment and confidence as you witness your progress. Embracing the principle of small changes allows you to build a solid foundation for continuous growth and development.

The Compound Effect

Consider the image of a small snowball rolling down a hill. As it continues, it gathers more snow and grows larger and larger. This is the compound effect in action. Tiny habit shifts operate in the same manner. Every small change you make adds up, resulting in significant progress over time. This accumulation of minor improvements can result in remarkable outcomes, illustrating the power of consistent, incremental adjustments.

The compound effect demonstrates how small actions, repeated consistently, can have a profound impact. As each small change reinforces and amplifies the others, the overall effect becomes increasingly substantial. This process highlights the importance of patience and persistence, as the benefits of tiny habit shifts become more evident and impactful over time.

By understanding and leveraging the compound effect, you can harness the power of small changes to achieve your long-term goals. This approach emphasizes the value of steady, continuous improvement, encouraging you to stay committed to your habits and trust in the process of gradual transformation.

Why Small Changes Work

1. **Less Resistance :** Small changes are less intimidating and easier to implement. They fit into your existing routine with minimal disruption. When changes are manageable, you are more likely to adopt and sustain them, reducing the risk of feeling overwhelmed or discouraged by the prospect of significant alterations to your lifestyle.

1. **Consistency :** Small shifts are easier to stick with, fostering consistency, which is key to habit formation. Consistency is key when forming new habits because it strengthens the behavior, making it a seamless part of your routine. By making small changes, you enhance your ability to maintain these habits over the long term.

3. **Momentum :** Each small success boosts your confidence and motivation, creating momentum for further changes. Achieving small wins offers positive reinforcement, motivating you to keep improving. This momentum builds upon itself, driving you toward greater achievements and fostering a sense of accomplishment and progress.

How to Start Implementing Tiny Habit Shifts ?

1. Start Small and Be Specific

Divide your goals into the smallest possible steps. Starting with smaller changes makes it easier to begin and maintain new habits over time. By concentrating on small, manageable changes, you lessen the intimidation and boost the chances of maintaining the new habit.

•Example: Instead of committing to reading for an hour every day, start with just 5 minutes. Gradually increase the time as the habit becomes ingrained. This approach allows you to build a reading habit without feeling overwhelmed, making it more sustainable and easier to integrate into your daily schedule.

Starting small and being specific sets a clear, achievable path toward your goals. It eliminates the pressure of drastic changes and promotes steady, continuous progress. Each small step you take reinforces the habit, making it a natural part of your routine over time.

2. Anchor New Habits to Existing Ones

Leverage existing habits as triggers for your new habits. This technique, known as habit stacking, leverages your current routines to build new ones. By associating a new habit with an established one, you create a reliable trigger that prompts the desired behavior.

•Example: If you want to start meditating, do it right after your morning coffee. The existing habit (drinking coffee) serves as a trigger for the new habit (meditating). This association helps you remember to meditate and seamlessly integrates it into your morning routine.

Anchoring new habits to existing ones simplifies the process of habit formation. It utilizes the natural flow of your daily activities to reinforce new behaviors, making it easier to establish and maintain them consistently. Habit stacking creates a structured and predictable environment for habit development.

3. Make It Easy

Remove obstacles that make it difficult to stick to your new habit. Simplify the process as much as possible to ensure that the habit is convenient and accessible. By minimizing barriers, you increase the likelihood of following through with your intentions.

•Example: If you want to eat healthier, keep fruits and vegetables prepped and within easy reach. This makes it easier to choose what's healthy. By making healthy options readily available, you make it easier to choose them over less nutritious alternatives.

Making it easy involves streamlining your environment and routine to support your new habits. When the desired behavior is convenient and effortless, you are more likely to engage in it regularly. This strategy eliminates excuses and facilitates consistent habit formation.

4. Direct your attention to one habit at a time

Avoid the temptation to change everything at once. Focusing on one habit at a time increases your chances of success. Concentrating your efforts allows you to dedicate sufficient attention and resources to establishing each habit thoroughly.

•Example: If your goal is to improve your sales performance, start by focusing solely on the habit of following up with clients. Once this habit is established, move on to the next one. This focused approach ensures that you build a strong foundation for each habit before introducing additional changes.

Focusing on one habit at a time prevents overwhelm and promotes sustainable habit development. It enables you to master each behavior individually, ensuring that new habits are solidified before adding more. This methodical approach fosters long-term success and consistency.

5. Track Your Progress

Keep a record of your habit shifts to monitor your progress and stay motivated. Use a journal, app, or simple checklist to track your daily actions. Tracking your habits provides tangible evidence of your efforts and achievements.

•Example: Try using a habit-tracking app to record how much time you spend reading each day. Observing your progress visually can provide significant motivation. It offers a clear view of your consistency and highlights areas where you may need to improve.

Monitoring your progress strengthens your dedication to your goals. It serves as a reminder of your dedication and helps keep your momentum going. Regularly reviewing your progress encourages you to stay on track and adjust your approach as needed.

6. Celebrate Small Wins

Acknowledge and celebrate your small successes. Positive reinforcement helps to strengthen the new habit and encourages you to keep going. Celebrating and Recognizing accomplishments, even minor ones, enhances your motivation and builds confidence.

•Example: Treat yourself to something enjoyable (like a favorite snack or a short break) when you complete a week of sticking to your new habit. These rewards provide immediate gratification and reinforce the positive behavior.

Celebrating small wins cultivates a positive mindset and reinforces your commitment to your goals. It creates a sense of accomplishment and motivates you to continue making progress. By recognizing and rewarding your efforts, you build a supportive environment for sustained habit formation.

Examples of Implementing Tiny Habit Shifts

To illustrate the power of tiny habit shifts, here are some real-life examples of small changes that can lead to significant improvements in professional performance. These examples demonstrate how minor adjustments can create substantial impacts when consistently applied over time.

Example 1: Enhancing Productivity

- **Goa l:** Increase daily productivity.

- **Tiny Habit Shift :** Begin your day by jotting down the three most crucial tasks to accomplish.

- **Impact :** This small change helps prioritize tasks, reduce overwhelm, and focus efforts on what matters most.

Breaking down productivity goals into manageable tasks each day can significantly boost overall performance. By identifying and noting the three most crucial tasks every morning, you create a clear roadmap for your day.Beginning your day with a clear plan can significantly improve how you organize your time and resources. This habit minimizes distractions, ensuring your energy is directed towards high-priority activities. Over time, it not only enhances productivity but also fosters a sense of accomplishment and progress. It reduces the likelihood of becoming overwhelmed by an extensive to-do list and provides a structured approach to tackling tasks. This habit shift emphasizes the importance of clarity and intention, setting a positive tone for the entire day. By consistently prioritizing tasks, you develop a disciplined routine that drives productivity and efficiency.

Example 2: Improving Communication Skills

- **Goal :** Become a better communicator.

- **Tiny Habit Shift :** Practice active listening by summarizing what others say before responding.

•**Impact :** This habit fosters better understanding, reduces miscommunication, and builds stronger relationships.

Attentive listening is a crucial skill for effective communication. By summarizing what others say before responding, you ensure that you fully understand their message. This small but powerful habit shift enhances clarity and reduces the chances of miscommunication. It shows respect for the speaker, demonstrating that you value their input and are genuinely engaged in the conversation. Over time, this practice can significantly strengthen your professional relationships and improve collaborative efforts.

Implementing active listening techniques can transform your interactions. It creates an environment where open communication thrives, fostering mutual respect and understanding. By making a conscious effort to listen actively, you enhance your ability to connect with others and respond thoughtfully. This habit shift not only improves communication skills but also builds a foundation of trust and collaboration, essential for professional success.

Example 3: Boosting Sales Performance

•**Goal :** Increase sales.

•**Tiny Habit Shift :** Follow up with one client every day.

•**Impact :** Regular follow-ups can significantly increase client engagement and conversion rates.

Consistent follow-ups are crucial for maintaining strong client relationships and boosting sales performance. By making it a habit to follow up with one client each day, you ensure that no potential opportunities are overlooked. This small, daily action keeps you engaged with your clients, addressing their needs and reinforcing your commitment to their success. Over time, regular follow-ups can lead to increased client satisfaction and higher conversion rates, driving your sales performance to new heights.

Regular follow-ups establish a systematic approach to client engagement. It demonstrates your dedication and reliability, fostering trust and loyalty among your clients. This habit shift ensures that you stay top-of-mind with your clients, enhancing your ability to identify and capitalize on new opportunities. By prioritizing consistent communication, you build a strong foundation for long-term client relationships and sustained sales growth.

Example 4: Enhancing Professional Development

•**Goal :** Continuously improve skills.

•**Tiny Habit Shift :** Spend 10 minutes each day reading industry-related articles or books.

•**Impact :** Consistent learning leads to staying updated with industry trends and improving expertise.

For professional growth and development, continuous learning is essential. By dedicating just 10 minutes each day to reading industry-related articles or books, you stay informed about the latest trends and advancements in your field. This small, daily commitment accumulates over time, significantly enhancing your knowledge and expertise. Regular learning keeps you competitive and adaptable, equipping you with the insights and skills needed to excel in your profession.

Allocating a few minutes each day to professional development can have a profound impact on your career trajectory. It ensures that you remain engaged with the evolving landscape of your industry, positioning yourself as a knowledgeable and proactive professional. This change in habit encourages a culture of ongoing improvement, nurturing a growth mindset that supports sustained success. By consistently investing in your learning, you enhance your ability to innovate and excel in your career.

Example 5: Reducing Stress

•**Goal :** Manage stress effectively.

•**Tiny Habit Shift** : Take a 5-minute break to practice deep breathing or mindfulness every afternoon.

•**Impact** : Taking regular breaks to relax lowers stress levels and boosts focus and productivity.

Effectively handling stress is essential for sustaining overall well-being and productivity levels. By incorporating a 5-minute break for deep breathing or mindfulness practice every afternoon, you create a powerful tool for stress reduction. This small, daily habit helps calm the mind, regulate emotions, and improve focus. Regular relaxation breaks provide a mental reset, allowing you to approach tasks with renewed energy and clarity. Over time, this practice can significantly enhance your ability to manage stress and maintain peak performance.

Integrating mindfulness or deep breathing exercises into your daily routine can transform your approach to stress management. These practices promote relaxation and mental clarity, reducing the negative impact of stress on your productivity and well-being. This habit shift emphasizes the importance of self-care and mental health, ensuring that you remain balanced and focused. By prioritizing regular relaxation breaks, you enhance your resilience and capacity to handle challenges effectively.

What We Discovered ?

Making tiny habit shifts is a powerful strategy for achieving professional excellence. By focusing on small, manageable changes, you can build momentum and make consistent progress toward your goals. The principle of small changes, combined with practical strategies and real-life examples, provides a roadmap for integrating new habits into your daily routine. Remember, it's the tiny shifts that, over time, lead to transformative results. In the next chapter, we will explore how to sustain these new habits and ensure they become a permanent part of your professional life. We'll move forward on this journey together, advancing gradually with each small step.

Embracing the power of tiny habit shifts is a profound approach to professional development. Instead of feeling overwhelmed by the prospect of significant changes, you can focus on making small, manageable adjustments that are easier to maintain. These small changes, though they may seem insignificant at first, gradually accumulate and lead to substantial progress. Consistency and a willingness to make incremental improvements are key. By integrating these small habits into your daily routine, you create a sustainable pathway to professional excellence.

The principle of small changes highlights the importance of starting with what is achievable. It emphasizes that you don't need to make drastic overhauls to see meaningful results. Instead, by implementing practical strategies such as starting small, anchoring new habits to existing ones, and tracking your progress, you can steadily advance toward your goals. Real-life examples illustrate how these strategies have been successfully applied by others, providing inspiration and a clear framework for your own journey. The power of small changes lies in their ability to build a solid foundation for lasting transformation.

As you focus on making tiny habit shifts, remember that the cumulative effect of these small adjustments can lead to significant outcomes. Each tiny shift contributes to building a strong and sustainable habit, reinforcing your commitment to professional growth. This method not only simplifies habit formation but also makes it more enjoyable and rewarding. In the next chapter, we will delve into strategies for sustaining these new habits, ensuring that they become a permanent part of your professional life. Together, we will continue this journey, one small step at a time, steadily moving closer to achieving your goals and realizing your full potential.

Unlocking Success: The 1% Rule and Compound Interest

The 1% rule, exemplified by the success of the British Cycling team under Sir Dave Brailsford, underscores the profound impact of marginal gains. This strategy focuses on making small, 1% improvements across various aspects of performance, which collectively lead to significant overall enhancement. This concept beautifully aligns with Albert Einstein's awe-inspiring principle of compound interest, which he hailed as the "eighth wonder of the world." Just as small amounts of interest accumulate over time to create substantial wealth, these minute, consistent enhancements in your habits and processes can compound to yield remarkable outcomes. Scientific research supports this, revealing that sustained incremental changes lead to exponential growth and unparalleled success. Each small gain, like a drop in a bucket, not only improves specific results but also builds momentum, fosters a culture of continuous improvement, and ultimately drives significant professional and personal achievements. Embrace the power of the 1% rule and compound interest, and unlock the path to your ultimate success.

Did You Know ?

The notion of "micro habits" revolves around the idea that tiny changes, which can be completed in less than 2 minutes, have the power to drive substantial transformation. This concept was brought into the spotlight by James Clear in his influential book "Atomic Habits." Clear's work emphasizes that these small, almost effortless actions, while appearing trivial in isolation, can accumulate to produce remarkable shifts in behavior and performance when practiced consistently.

In "Atomic Habits," James Clear elaborates on how integrating these micro habits into your daily routine can be a game-changer. The beauty of micro habits lies in their simplicity and the minimal time commitment they require. For instance, reading a single page of a book or doing two push-ups might not seem impactful on their own, but these tiny actions, performed regularly, create a foundation for larger behavioral changes. Over time, these micro habits build momentum, making it easier to adopt more substantial habits and achieve your broader goals.

The concept of micro habits is powerful because it leverages the principle of making small, manageable changes to instigate significant improvements. By focusing on actions that take less than 2 minutes, you reduce the resistance and procrastination often associated with starting new habits. This approach not only makes it easier to incorporate new behaviors into your routine but also ensures that these behaviors are sustainable. As these micro habits become ingrained, they pave the way for more significant habit changes, ultimately leading to enhanced performance and achievement.

Chapter 5:
Implementing Daily Habit Changes

"Implementation turns intentions into accomplishments."

This chapter highlights the crucial role of starting small, emphasizing that manageable steps are more sustainable and effective. Concentrating on one habit at a time helps you avoid the overwhelm that typically comes with drastic changes. We will also discuss the significance of prioritizing consistency over intensity, as regular, smaller efforts can lead to more enduring results. Additionally, this chapter will introduce various tools and methods for tracking your progress, ensuring that you stay motivated and on course for continuous growth and development.

Starting Small: One Habit at a Time

One Habit at a Time emphasizes the effectiveness of focusing on a single habit rather than attempting to change multiple behaviors simultaneously. This approach is rooted in the understanding that human willpower and motivation are finite resources. Focusing on a single habit allows you to dedicate your full attention and effort to mastering it, making the process less intimidating and more manageable. This focused approach also allows you to experience the satisfaction of small victories, which can boost your confidence and encourage you to continue on your path of habit formation.

Beginning with a single habit provides a clear and attainable goal, reducing the likelihood of becoming discouraged by the slow progress or setbacks that can occur when trying to change too much at once. This method promotes a sense of control and accomplishment, as you can clearly see the impact of your efforts. Over time, as this new habit becomes ingrained in your routine, you can gradually introduce additional habits, building upon your initial success and creating a sustainable pattern of growth and improvement.

By starting small and concentrating on one habit at a time, you lay a solid foundation for long-term change. This approach ensures that each new habit is given the attention and consistency it needs to become a permanent part of your routine. As you continue to build on these small, incremental changes, you create a cumulative effect that leads to significant and lasting transformation. This method not only makes the process of habit change more manageable but also sets you up for continued success in achieving your professional and personal goals.

The Power of Focus

The Power of Focus lies in its ability to streamline your efforts towards mastering a single habit. When you concentrate on one specific behavior, you can allocate all your mental and physical resources towards perfecting it. This focused approach minimizes distractions and prevents the dispersion of your energy across multiple tasks, which often leads to burnout and decreased effectiveness. By honing in on one habit, you create a clear path for consistent practice and improvement, setting the stage for lasting change. This strategy not only simplifies the process of habit formation but also significantly boosts your chances of achieving long-term success.

Focusing on a single habit allows you to develop a deep understanding of the factors that contribute to its success or failure. You can experiment with different techniques, track your progress meticulously, and make necessary adjustments without the added complexity of juggling multiple changes. This concentrated effort helps you to identify and overcome obstacles more effectively, leading to a stronger and more resilient habit. Over time, as this habit becomes second nature, you build a solid foundation that supports the addition of new habits, creating a domino effect of positive change in your life.

Furthermore, the power of focus fosters a sense of achievement and motivation. As you see tangible progress in mastering a single habit, your confidence grows, reinforcing your commitment to continue. This positive reinforcement fuels your drive to maintain and expand your efforts, creating a cycle of success that propels you towards your larger goals. By focusing on one habit at a time, you harness the full potential of your willpower and dedication, ensuring that each new behavior becomes a permanent and beneficial part of your daily routine.

Example : Morning Routine illustrates the practical application of starting small and focusing on a single habit. Imagine your goal is to integrate regular exercise into your morning routine. Instead of aiming for an hour-long workout from the get-go, which can be daunting and unsustainable, begin with a manageable five-minute exercise session each day. This small commitment makes it easier to stick with the habit, as it requires minimal effort and can be easily integrated into your existing schedule. By consistently performing this brief workout, you lay the groundwork for a more extensive exercise regimen, making it a natural and enjoyable part of your morning routine.

As this initial five-minute workout becomes a habitual part of your mornings, you can start to gradually increase both the duration and intensity of your exercise sessions. This incremental approach ensures that your body and mind adapt to the new routine without feeling overwhelmed. Over time, those extra minutes add up, transforming your short, manageable workout into a comprehensive fitness routine. This method not only builds physical endurance and strength but also fosters a sense of accomplishment and motivation, encouraging you to maintain and expand your efforts.

The gradual progression of your morning exercise routine exemplifies the power of focus and the effectiveness of starting small. By dedicating yourself to a brief yet consistent practice, you establish a strong foundation for long-term success. This approach can be applied to any habit you wish to develop, demonstrating that small, focused changes can lead to significant improvements in behavior and performance. As you continue to build upon this routine, you establish a sustainable and rewarding habit that supports your overall health and well-being.

Consistency Over Intensity

Consistency Over Intensity underscores the fundamental principle that sustained, regular effort is more effective than intermittent, high-intensity bursts when it comes to forming new habits. The allure of pushing yourself to the maximum can be strong, especially when you're eager to see quick results. However, this approach often leads to burnout and inconsistency, which can derail your progress. Instead, focusing on maintaining a steady, consistent practice, even if it's not perfect, builds a reliable routine that becomes ingrained over time. This steady approach helps you develop a habit that is sustainable, reducing the risk of giving up due to exhaustion or frustration.

Consistency is key because it helps establish a routine that your brain can recognize and follow. Engaging in a habit every day, even if it's just for a few minutes, reinforces the behavior and makes it a natural part of your daily life. This daily repetition strengthens the neural pathways associated with the habit, making it easier to perform the behavior automatically in the future. The small, daily efforts add up, creating a cumulative effect that leads to significant progress over time. By prioritizing consistency, you ensure that the habit becomes a stable and enduring part of your routine.

Moreover, consistency builds resilience and discipline. When you commit to practicing a habit every day, you learn to overcome obstacles and resist the urge to skip days, even when you're tired or unmotivated. This persistence fosters a sense of accomplishment and self-discipline, which can be applied to other areas of your life. By embracing consistency over intensity, you develop a mindset that values steady progress and long-term success. This approach not only helps you achieve your immediate goals but also lays the foundation for continued growth and improvement.

The Habit Loop

The Habit Loop describes the neurological process underlying habit formation, comprising three elements: the cue, the routine, and the reward. When you consistently engage in a behavior, you repeatedly activate this loop, reinforcing the neural pathways involved. The cue triggers your brain to initiate the routine, and the reward provides a sense of satisfaction, encouraging the repetition of the behavior. This consistent activation strengthens the neural connections in your brain, making the habit more automatic and easier to execute. By understanding and leveraging the habit loop, you can create a powerful mechanism for developing and maintaining new habits.

The cue is the initial trigger that signals your brain to start the habit. It could be a particular time of day, a certain emotional state, or an environmental condition. Consistently responding to the same cue helps reinforce a strong association between the trigger and the behavior. The routine refers to the specific behavior or action you carry out in reaction to the cue. Repeating this routine consistently reinforces the behavior, making it more ingrained in your daily life. The reward is the positive result or satisfaction you feel upon finishing the routine. Rewards can be of various types. Like,

1. The reward is the sense of achievement or happiness you experience after completing the routine.

2. Completing the routine brings a feeling of satisfaction or a positive outcome as your reward.

3. The satisfaction or positive result you get from finishing the routine is the reward.

4. After finishing the routine, the positive result or feeling of satisfaction is your reward.

5. The reward comes in the form of positive feelings or a sense of accomplishment once the routine is finished.

By consistently engaging in a habit, you create a positive feedback loop that strengthens the behavior. Each repetition of the habit loop strengthens the neural pathways in your brain, making the habit more automatic and reducing the need for conscious effort. This consistency builds momentum, making it easier to maintain the habit over time. Understanding the habit loop and focusing on consistency allows you to leverage the natural mechanisms of habit formation, creating a strong foundation for lasting change.

Lets see an Example : Daily Writing

Suppose you aim to enhance your writing abilities. Instead of setting an overwhelming goal like writing for hours every day, start with a manageable commitment: writing just 100 words daily. This small, consistent effort may seem insignificant, but it plays a crucial role in reinforcing the habit. By writing a little each day, you create a routine that becomes second nature. Over time, this daily practice not only solidifies the habit but also improves your writing skills as you gradually become more comfortable and proficient with each session.

This approach of writing 100 words daily ensures that you maintain a regular writing practice without feeling overwhelmed. The consistency helps you overcome the inertia of starting and keeps you engaged in the habit, even on days when you feel less motivated. As the habit becomes ingrained, you can gradually increase your word count, expanding your writing sessions naturally without additional pressure. This incremental growth ensures that your writing skills develop steadily, building confidence and competence over time.

Consistently engaging in this small act of writing also fosters creativity and discipline. By making writing a daily habit, you train your mind to generate ideas and express them regularly. This regular practice helps you overcome writer's block and enhances your ability to articulate thoughts clearly and effectively. The habit of daily writing not only improves your technical skills but also cultivates a disciplined mindset that can be applied to other areas of your professional and personal life. By focusing on small, consistent efforts, you achieve meaningful progress and develop a sustainable writing practice that supports your long-term goals.

Tools for Tracking Progress

Monitoring your progress is crucial for accountability and maintaining motivation. Fortunately, there are many tools and techniques available to help you monitor your habits and measure your growth.

Habit Tracking Apps

Habit tracking apps, such as Habitica or Streaks, allow you to set goals, track your progress, and receive reminders to stay on track. These apps provide valuable insights into your habits and help you identify areas for improvement.

Journaling

Keeping a habit journal can also be an effective way to track your progress and reflect on your experiences. Use your journal to record your daily activities, track your successes and setbacks, and identify patterns over time.

Accountability Partners

Partnering with a friend or family member can provide additional accountability and support on your habit change journey. Discuss your goals with a trusted person and have regular conversations about your progress and obstacles.

What We Discovered ?

Implementing daily habit changes is essential for achieving lasting success in your personal and professional life. By starting small, prioritizing consistency over intensity, and utilizing tools for tracking progress, you can build the habits necessary to reach your goals. Remember, change takes time and effort, but with dedication and perseverance, you can create a life filled with purpose, productivity, and fulfillment. In the next chapter, we will explore strategies for overcoming common obstacles and staying on course as you continue your habit change journey.

Did You Know?

On average, it requires 66 days for a new behavior to become automatic. This statistic highlights the significance of maintaining consistency and exercising patience when you're trying to establish new habits. Understanding this timeline is essential because it sets realistic expectations and helps you stay committed to the process, even when progress seems slow. By knowing that it typically takes around two months for a habit to become ingrained, you can approach habit formation with the right mindset, prepared for a journey that requires persistence and dedication.

This research finding underscores the power of committing to small, consistent actions over an extended period. Instead of aiming for immediate, drastic changes, focus on making manageable adjustments that you can sustain daily. Each small step you take is a building block that gradually reshapes your behavior and strengthens the neural pathways in your brain associated with the new habit. By consistently repeating the behavior, you are effectively rewiring your brain, making the habit more automatic and easier to maintain in the long run. This process of gradual, consistent effort is key to achieving lasting change and integrating new habits into your daily routine.

Consistency and patience are crucial beyond measure. It's natural to feel discouraged if progress appears slow at first, but remember that every small step you take is a crucial part of the transformation. Each day you engage in the new behavior, you're reinforcing the habit loop and moving closer to making the behavior automatic. Embrace the journey and trust the process, knowing that with time and persistence, your efforts will pay off. By maintaining a steady, consistent approach, you can achieve your goals and create lasting changes that support your professional and personal growth.

Chapter 6
Overcoming Challenges and Obstacles

"Conquering challenges sets the stage for

your future achievements."

Every journey toward professional excellence encounters its fair share of challenges and obstacles. Encountering challenges is a natural aspect of growth and development. They arise when you stretch beyond your comfort zone and aim for new achievements. It's important to understand that encountering obstacles is not a sign of failure but rather an indication that you are moving forward. Each challenge presents an opportunity to learn, adapt, and become stronger. Embracing this mindset will help you navigate difficulties with resilience and determination, ultimately propelling you toward your goals.

To overcome obstacles, the first step is acknowledging their existence. Pretending that challenges do not exist or ignoring them can derail your progress and diminish your motivation. Once you recognize the barriers, take proactive steps to address them.

Identifying Common Barriers

Understanding the common barriers that can impede habit formation is the first step in overcoming them. Here are some typical challenges you might face:

1. Lack of Time

One of the most frequent excuses for not sticking to new habits is the perceived lack of time. Our busy schedules often seem incompatible with the commitment required to establish new routines. Lack of time is a pervasive issue in today's fast-paced world. Many people feel overwhelmed by their daily responsibilities and believe they simply don't have enough time to devote to new habits. This perception can be a significant barrier to habit formation.

2. Lack of Motivation

Motivation can fluctuate, making it difficult to maintain new habits consistently. Without a strong, intrinsic reason for why a habit is important, it's easy to lose interest. Motivation is a key driver of behavior change, but it can be unpredictable. Even with the best intentions, your motivation levels can wane over time, especially if the new habit doesn't immediately yield visible results.

3. Environmental Triggers

Sometimes, our surroundings and routines can create barriers. Lack of a supportive environment can impede your progress in adopting the new habit. Your environment plays a significant role in shaping your behavior.Not having surroundings that support your new habits can make it hard to keep them up. Environmental triggers, such as cluttered spaces, lack of resources, or unsupportive people, can impede your progress.

Techniques for Staying on Track

Once you've identified potential barriers, it's essential to have strategies in place to stay on track. Understanding the obstacles you might face is only half the battle; having actionable strategies to overcome these challenges is crucial for success. Establishing a robust plan ensures you're prepared to deal with difficulties as they arise. With the right techniques, you can maintain your momentum and keep your new habits on track, even when faced with setbacks. Embracing this proactive strategy cultivates resilience and nurtures a positive mindset, empowering you to effectively manage the highs and lows of habit formation.

Here are some techniques to help you maintain your habits: Implementing practical strategies is vital for sustaining new habits. These techniques provide a framework for integrating new behaviors into your routine, ensuring they become a lasting part of your daily life. Each method offers a unique way to address common barriers, providing you with the tools needed to stay committed to your goals. Using these approaches enables you to build a nurturing environment that promotes both consistency and growth. Let's explore these strategies in detail to understand how they can help you stay on track with your new habits.

1. Break Down Goals - Divide your overarching goal into smaller, more manageable tasks. This approach makes the task seem less overwhelming and more within reach Breaking down your goals into smaller steps helps reduce overwhelm and makes it easier to take consistent action. Instead of focusing on the entire goal, which can seem insurmountable, you tackle it piece by piece. This approach allows you to build momentum gradually, celebrating small victories along the way. By setting smaller, attainable targets, you create a sense of progress and achievement that motivates you to keep moving forward.

Example : Gradual Exercise Routine - If your goal is to exercise for 30 minutes daily, start with just 10 minutes and gradually increase the duration as the habit becomes more ingrained. This step-by-step approach simplifies the integration of new habits into your daily routine. Starting small reduces the initial resistance and helps you establish a consistent practice. As you become more comfortable with the habit, you can slowly increase the intensity or duration, making the change feel more natural and less overwhelming.

2. Use Reminders and Triggers - Set reminders and create triggers that prompt you to perform your new habit. This helps reinforce the habit loop and keeps you accountable. Reminders and triggers act as cues that prompt you to engage in the desired behavior. These cues can be physical, such as placing your workout clothes where you can see them, or digital, like setting reminders on your devices. By associating the new habit with an existing routine or specific time, you make it easier to remember and perform the action consistently.

Example : Digital Reminders - Use your smartphone or computer to set daily reminders for your new habit, like a pop-up notification to remind you to practice deep breathing exercises. Digital reminders are an effective way to prompt you to take action. They provide timely nudges that help you stay on track with your new habits. By setting consistent reminders, you reinforce the habit loop, making it more likely that the new behavior will become automatic over time.

3. Find an Accountability Partner - Having someone to share your progress with can provide motivation and support. An accountability partner can offer encouragement and hold you responsible for your commitments. Partnering with someone who shares similar goals creates a sense of shared responsibility and motivation. This mutual support system helps you stay committed to your habits, as you have someone to celebrate successes with and discuss challenges. The presence of an accountability partner adds a layer of external motivation that can be incredibly effective in maintaining consistency.

Example : Study Buddy - Pair up with a colleague who has similar goals. Maintain regular communication to share successes and address difficulties. Having a study buddy or accountability partner keeps you motivated and on track. Regular check-ins provide an opportunity to reflect on your progress, address any difficulties, and receive encouragement. This collaborative approach fosters a sense of community and shared purpose, making it easier to stay committed to your new habits.

3. Find an Accountability Partner - Having someone to share your progress with can provide motivation and support. An accountability partner can offer encouragement and hold you responsible for your commitments. Partnering with someone who shares similar goals creates a sense of shared responsibility and motivation. This mutual support system helps you stay committed to your habits, as you have someone to celebrate successes with and discuss challenges. The presence of an accountability partner adds a layer of external motivation that can be incredibly effective in maintaining consistency.

Example : Study Buddy - Pair up with a colleague who has similar goals. Maintain regular communication to share successes and address difficulties. Having a study buddy or accountability partner keeps you motivated and on track. Regular check-ins provide an opportunity to reflect on your progress, address any difficulties, and receive encouragement. This collaborative approach fosters a sense of community and shared purpose, making it easier to stay committed to your new habits.

4. Celebrate Small Wins - Give yourself credit for small wins and celebrate them as they happen. Celebrating these milestones can boost your motivation and reinforce the positive behavior. Celebrating small wins creates a positive feedback loop that reinforces the new behavior. Acknowledging your progress, no matter how minor, boosts your morale and encourages you to continue. Rewards don't have to be extravagant; even simple acts of self-appreciation can make a significant impact on your motivation and commitment.

Example : Create a structured reward system to encourage yourself as you reach milestones. For instance, treat yourself to something enjoyable after a week of consistently following your new habit. Establishing a reward system provides an incentive to maintain your new habits. By linking your efforts to a positive outcome, you make the process more enjoyable and motivating. This approach helps sustain your motivation over the long term, making it easier to integrate the new habit into your daily routine.

Adjusting Your Approach as Needed

Being adaptable is critical for habit development. In the journey of building new habits, being adaptable is key to long-term success. Rigidly sticking to a plan that isn't yielding results can lead to frustration and burnout. Instead, embrace a mindset that is adaptable to making necessary adjustments. This flexibility enables you to stay resilient in the face of challenges and ensures that your habit-building process remains dynamic and responsive to your needs. Remember, the focus is on progress, not achieving perfection.

If a particular approach isn't working, don't be afraid to adjust it. Recognize that not all strategies will work for everyone. If you find yourself struggling with a specific method, it's perfectly okay to pivot and try something different. The willingness to adapt your approach is a strength, not a setback. This adaptability allows you to discover what works best for you, ensuring that your new habits can be sustained over the long term. Let's explore some practical ways to adjust your strategies effectively.

To adapt your strategies, try these steps: Refining your habit formation approach will increase your success rate. Each step provides a practical way to evaluate and adjust your methods, ensuring that your habits remain aligned with your goals and circumstances. Whether it's reevaluating your objectives, experimenting with new techniques, or seeking external feedback, these strategies offer a comprehensive guide to maintaining flexibility in your habit-building journey.

1. Reevaluate Your Goals - Sometimes, the initial goal might be too ambitious or not aligned with your current circumstances. Reflect on and alter your goals to make them more practical. Consistently reassessing your goals is key to ensuring they stay relevant and within reach. Life circumstances change, and what seemed like a reasonable goal initially might become overwhelming over time. By reevaluating your goals, you can align them with your current capabilities and resources, making them more attainable and less stressful.

Example : Realistic Deadlines - If you aimed to read one book per week but find it overwhelming, adjust your goal to one book every two weeks. This adjustment acknowledges the reality of your schedule and reduces unnecessary pressure. By setting a more manageable target, you create a sustainable habit that fits better into your routine. This way, you can enjoy the process of reading without feeling rushed, ensuring a more enjoyable and productive experience.

2. Experiment with Different Methods - If one method isn't yielding results, try a different approach. Experimenting with various techniques can help you find what works best for you. Being open to new methods is vital for finding the most effective strategies for your habit-building process. Different approaches work for different people, so don't hesitate to try alternative techniques. This experimentation allows you to tailor your methods to your unique preferences and circumstances, increasing the likelihood of success.

Example : Alternative Study Techniques - If you're struggling with traditional study methods, try incorporating multimedia resources like videos or podcasts into your learning routine. Shifting to this approach can make learning more interactive and approachable. By exploring different formats, you can find the ones that resonate most with you, making the learning process more enjoyable and effective. This adaptability ensures that your study habits are both productive and sustainable.

3. Seek Feedback - Get feedback from others to gain different perspectives on your progress. Insightful criticism can help you spot areas to develop. Seeking feedback provides valuable insights that you might not notice on your own. External perspectives can highlight blind spots and offer suggestions for enhancement. Embracing constructive criticism helps you refine your habits and strategies, ensuring continuous improvement and growth.

Example : Peer Reviews - Ask a trusted colleague or mentor to review your progress and provide feedback on how you can enhance your habit-building strategies. Regular reviews with a mentor or peer can offer new insights and keep you accountable. These discussions can help you stay focused and motivated, providing valuable guidance on how to optimize your approach. By incorporating feedback, you can make informed adjustments that drive better results.

What We Discovered ?

Overcoming challenges and obstacles is an integral part of achieving professional excellence. By identifying common barriers, employing techniques to stay on track, and adjusting your approach as needed, you can navigate through difficulties and maintain your commitment to new habits. Keep in mind, professional growth is a long-term journey, not a quick race. Remain determined, stay adaptable, and continue progressing. In the next chapter, we will explore how to sustain your new habits and make them a permanent part of your professional life. Together, we'll continue to transform small changes into significant achievements.

Did You Know?

Research from the University of Scranton indicates that only 8% of people achieve their New Year's goals, largely due to a lack of planning and flexibility. By identifying common barriers, employing effective strategies to stay on track, and adjusting your approach as needed, you significantly increase your chances of overcoming obstacles and successfully forming lasting habits.

Chapter 7
Reinforcing New Habits

"New habits flourish when nurtured with

consistency and commitment."

Once you've established new habits, the challenge lies in maintaining them over the long term. This chapter will explore how to build long-term consistency, the power of positive reinforcement, and the importance of celebrating small wins.

1. Building Long-Term Consistency

Long-term consistency is the cornerstone of lasting habit change. Establishing a habit is only the first step; maintaining it over time is where the real challenge lies. To ensure your new habits become permanent fixtures in your life, you need strategies that promote consistency and resilience.

Routine Integration

Integrate your new habits into your existing routines. When a new habit is seamlessly linked to an already established routine, it becomes significantly easier to maintain. This integration reduces the effort required to remember and practice the new habit, making it a natural part of your daily life.

Example : Morning Routine Integration

If your goal is to meditate daily, attach this habit to something you already do every morning, such as brewing your coffee. As soon as you finish making your coffee, take five minutes to meditate. By connecting meditation with your coffee routine, you create a seamless transition that helps solidify the new habit as part of your morning ritual.

Accountability Systems

Set up systems to hold yourself accountable. Whether through technology, social support, or personal tracking, accountability can help ensure you stick to your habits. Knowing that you have a system in place to track your progress and keep you on course can significantly boost your commitment and consistency.

Example : Habit-Tracking Apps

Use habit-tracking apps like Habitica or Loop Habit Tracker to monitor your progress. These apps offer features like reminders, visual progress reports, and streak tracking, all of which can help you stay on track. The visual representation of your progress serves as a constant motivator, reminding you of your commitments and encouraging you to maintain your new habits.

Continuous Learning and Adaptation

Stay informed about best practices and be willing to adjust your habits as needed. Continuous learning ensures that your habits remain relevant and effective, adapting to new circumstances and evolving goals. This proactive approach prevents your habits from becoming stale or obsolete.

Example : Professional Development

If your goal is to enhance your skills, continuously seek new resources, courses, or workshops related to your field. This ongoing learning will keep your skills sharp and your habits aligned with the latest industry standards. By regularly updating your knowledge and skills, you ensure that your habits remain beneficial and aligned with your professional growth.

Using Positive Reinforcement

Positive reinforcement is a powerful tool for strengthening new habits. By rewarding yourself for consistency, you create a positive feedback loop that encourages ongoing commitment. This reinforcement helps solidify the habit and makes it more likely that you will continue to perform the desired behavior over the long term.

Immediate Rewards

Providing yourself with small, immediate rewards for completing your habit is a highly effective way to reinforce the behavior. These rewards can be simple and personal, tailored to what you enjoy and what will motivate you to keep going. Immediate rewards create a direct connection between the habit and a positive outcome, making it more appealing to continue.

Example : Reward System

Create a list of small rewards that you enjoy and can easily access. For instance, allow yourself to watch an episode of your favorite show after completing a work task you've been avoiding. This immediate gratification helps build a positive association with the task, making it easier to tackle similar tasks in the future. Over time, these small rewards contribute to a sustained habit of productivity.

2. Social Reinforcement

Sharing your achievements with others can provide a significant motivational boost. Positive feedback and recognition from peers, friends, or family can be highly encouraging. Social reinforcement leverages the human need for social approval and support, making the habit-forming process more enjoyable and sustainable.

Example : Sharing Successes

Post your progress on social media or share updates with a supportive group. Receiving encouragement and congratulations from friends and colleagues can reinforce your commitment to your new habit. The public nature of sharing your progress adds an extra layer of accountability, as you are more likely to stick to your commitments when others are aware of them.

2. Visual Cues

Using visual reminders and positive affirmations to reinforce your habits can be highly motivating. Visual cues keep your goals and progress front and center, serving as constant reminders of what you are working towards. Regular visual reminders help sustain focus and motivation over the long term.

Example : Vision Boards

Put together a vision board featuring visuals and quotes aligned with your aspirations. Place it somewhere you'll see daily, such as your workspace or bedroom, to keep your aspirations front and center. Seeing these visual representations of your goals every day helps reinforce your commitment and reminds you of the reasons behind your efforts. Vision boards are powerful tools for keeping your long-term objectives in mind and maintaining motivation on a daily basis.

4. Celebrating Small Wins

Acknowledging small victories is essential for keeping up motivation and encouraging positive actions. Acknowledging your progress, no matter how minor, helps you stay motivated and focused on your long-term goals. This practice not only boosts your morale but also reinforces the effort you put into achieving your goals, making the journey toward professional excellence more rewarding and enjoyable.

1.Recognize Achievements

Taking the time to recognize and appreciate your achievements, no matter how small, is essential for maintaining a positive mindset. This recognition boosts your morale and reinforces the efforts you are putting into your new habits, making it easier to stay committed.

Example: Daily Reflection

At the end of each day, reflect on what you've accomplished, no matter how small. Write down these achievements in a journal to track your progress over time. This daily practice of reflection helps you see the cumulative effect of your efforts, reinforcing the positive behavior and encouraging you to continue.

5. Set Milestones

Breaking your larger goals into smaller, manageable milestones helps make the process of habit formation more attainable and less overwhelming. Celebrating each achievement maintains your motivation and offers a feeling of success that pushes you ahead.

Example: Learning a New Skill

If you're learning a new skill, set milestones such as completing a beginner course, creating a small project, or receiving positive feedback from a peer. Celebrate each milestone with a small reward, such as treating yourself to something you enjoy. These celebrations acknowledge your progress and keep you excited about reaching the next milestone.

6. Share Your Wins

Sharing your wins with others not only reinforces your own success but also inspires those around you. This social aspect of celebrating achievements can foster a supportive environment and motivate everyone to recognize and celebrate their own achievements.

Example: Team Celebrations

In a professional setting, share your small wins with your team. This can foster a supportive environment where everyone feels encouraged to acknowledge their own progress. For instance, during team meetings, take a moment to highlight individual achievements and celebrate these small victories together. This practice not only boosts individual morale but also strengthens team cohesion and motivation.

What We Discovered ?

Reinforcing new habits is essential for achieving lasting change. By building long-term consistency, using positive reinforcement, and celebrating small wins, you can ensure that your new habits become a permanent part of your professional and personal life. Remember, achieving professional excellence is a steady marathon, not a swift sprint. Stay focused, celebrate your milestones, and keep pushing ahead. In the next chapter, we will explore how to sustain your new habits and make them a permanent part of your professional life. Together, we'll continue to transform small changes into significant achievements.

Did You Know?

Research published in the *Journal of Personality and Social Psychology* found that people who tracked their progress toward goals were more likely to succeed. Keeping a record of your achievements, no matter how small, helps maintain motivation and provides a tangible reminder of your progress.

Chapter 8
Evaluating Progress and Adapting

"Progress is best measured through reflection

and the willingness to adapt."

The journey of habit formation doesn't end once a habit is established. Regular evaluation and adaptation are crucial to ensure your habits continue to serve your professional goals effectively. In this chapter, we'll delve into reflecting on your habit journey, measuring the impact on your professional goals, and adapting and refining your habits for sustained success.

Reflecting on Your Habit Journey

Reflecting on your experiences is a potent mechanism for both personal and professional advancement. Taking the time to reflect on your habit journey helps you understand what's working, what's not, and how you can improve. This process of introspection not only provides insights into your progress but also helps you stay motivated and focused on your long-term goals.

1. Regular Self-Assessment

Scheduling regular intervals to assess your progress is essential for staying on track and making necessary adjustments. Consistent self-assessment allows you to evaluate your habits, understand your successes, and identify areas for improvement.

Example: Weekly Reflection

Every Sunday evening, spend 15-30 minutes reflecting on your habits. Write down what you accomplished, the challenges you faced, and what you learned. This routine can provide valuable insights and keep you motivated. By regularly assessing your progress, you can make informed decisions about how to adjust your habits to better align with your goals.

2. Identifying Patterns

Looking for patterns in your behavior is crucial for understanding which habits were easier to adopt and which ones posed challenges. Identifying these patterns can help you develop strategies to overcome obstacles and reinforce successful behaviors.

Example: Tracking Patterns

Use a journal or app to track your habits daily. After a few weeks, review your entries to spot trends. For instance, you might notice that you struggle with your evening workout on days when you have back-to-back meetings. Recognizing such patterns can help you adjust your schedule or find alternative solutions to maintain consistency in your habits.

3. Celebrating Successes

Acknowledging and celebrating your successes, no matter how small, is vital for boosting morale and reinforcing the behavior you want to maintain. Positive reinforcement creates a cycle that inspires you to maintain your efforts.

Example: Personal Rewards

Create a reward system for yourself. After a month of consistent habit practice, treat yourself to something special, like a nice dinner or a relaxing day off. Celebrating these milestones not only recognizes your hard work but also provides motivation to keep progressing.

Measuring Impact on Professional Goals

Measuring the effectiveness of your habits helps confirm they are aiding your professional aims. This evaluation can help you understand the tangible benefits of your new habits, enabling you to make necessary adjustments and stay on track for success.

1. Setting Clear Metrics

Create definite standards to track the success of your habits. These metrics should be directly linked to your professional goals. Clear and specific metrics provide a concrete way to evaluate whether your habits are producing the desired results.

Example: Sales Metrics

If you're a sales executive, measure the impact of your new networking habit by tracking the number of new leads generated or the increase in closed deals over a specific period. Setting clear metrics such as these allows you to quantify the benefits of your habit and determine its effectiveness in reaching your professional objectives.

2. Gathering Feedback

Seek feedback from colleagues, mentors, or supervisors. Their perspective can provide valuable insights into the impact of your habits on your professional performance. Constructive feedback helps you understand how your habits are perceived and their effects on your work environment.

Example: Performance Reviews

During regular performance reviews, discuss the habits you've been working on and ask for feedback on how they have affected your work. Use this feedback to refine your approach. This dialogue not only helps you gauge the effectiveness of your habits but also strengthens your professional relationships and opens up opportunities for further improvement.

3. Analyzing Data

Collect and analyze data related to your habits. This data can help you identify correlations between your habits and your professional achievements. Analyzing objective data provides a factual basis for understanding the impact of your habits.

Example: Productivity Tracking

If you've implemented time management habits, use productivity tracking tools to analyze your efficiency. Compare your output before and after adopting the new habits to measure their impact. By examining data trends, you can determine which habits are most beneficial and make informed decisions about how to optimize your routines.

Adapting and Refining Your Habits

As your career goals and circumstances change, your habits may require modification. Being flexible and willing to adapt is key to maintaining their effectiveness. This chapter will explore how to reassess goals, experiment with new approaches, and seek continuous improvement to ensure your habits remain aligned with your evolving professional journey.

1. Reassessing Goals

Regularly review your career objectives to confirm your habits are still supporting them. As your career progresses, your priorities may shift, and your habits should reflect these changes. Reassessment allows you to stay focused on what truly matters and adjust your habits accordingly.

Example: Career Advancement

If you receive a promotion, reassess your goals and habits to align with your new responsibilities. Adapt your habits to support the skills and tasks required for your new role. For instance, if your new position demands more leadership skills, you might develop habits focused on team management and strategic planning.

2. Experimenting with New Approaches

Don't be afraid to experiment with new approaches if a habit isn't working as well as you hoped. Trying different methods can help you find more effective ways to achieve your goals. Trying new things fosters creativity and ensures your habits remain adaptable and tuned to your requirements.

Example: Time Management Techniques

If your current time management technique isn't yielding the desired results, experiment with other methods such as the Pomodoro Technique or time blocking to see if they work better for you. By exploring different strategies, you can discover what maximizes your productivity and efficiency.

3. Seeking Continuous Improvement

Adopt a mindset of continuous improvement. Always be on the lookout for ways to refine and enhance your habits to better support your professional growth. This approach ensures that your habits evolve with your career and remain relevant in a changing environment.

Example: Professional Development

Keep yourself updated on the latest trends and recommended practices within your profession. Attend workshops, read industry literature, and seek opportunities for continuous learning to keep your habits relevant and effective. Continuous professional development helps you stay competitive and ensures your habits contribute to your long-term success.

What We Discovered ?

Evaluating your progress and adapting your habits is crucial for sustaining professional growth. By reflecting on your habit journey, measuring their impact on your professional goals, and being willing to adapt and refine your approach, you can ensure that your habits continue to drive your success. Remember, the path to professional excellence is dynamic, requiring ongoing assessment and adjustment. In the next chapter, we will explore how to sustain your new habits and make them a permanent part of your professional life. Together, we'll continue to transform small changes into significant achievements.

Did You Know?

A study by the Harvard Business Review found that professionals who regularly reflect on their performance are 23% more productive than those who do not. Reflection helps you understand your strengths and weaknesses, making it easier to adapt and refine your habits for continuous improvement.

Understanding the Pomodoro Technique

The Pomodoro Technique, created by Francesco Cirillo in the late 1980s, is a widely recognized approach to enhancing time management. Named after the tomato-shaped kitchen timer that Cirillo used during university, the technique is designed to improve focus and productivity by breaking work into manageable, timed intervals.

How the Pomodoro Technique Works

1. Choose a Task : Start by selecting a specific task you want to work on.

2. Set the timer : Set the timer for a duration of 25 minutes. This period is referred to as one "Pomodoro."

3. Work : Focus solely on the task until the timer goes off. Minimize distractions and engage fully in the task at hand.

4. Short Break : Take a 5-minute break after the timer rings. Allowing this momentary pause helps your brain rest and re-energize.

5. Repeat : Repeat the cycle of 25 minutes of focused work followed by a 5-minute break. Complete four cycles.

6. Long Break : Once you've completed four Pomodoros, allow yourself a longer break of 15-30 minutes. This extended rest helps to consolidate your focus and energy for the next set of Pomodoros.

Benefits of the Pomodoro Technique

4. Enhances Focus and Concentration

5. Reduces Burnout

6. Improves Time Management

7. Provides a Structured Workday

Chapter 9
Sustaining and Scaling Habits

"To scale habits, nurture them with the same

dedication that helped you start."

Building new habits is a significant achievement, but maintaining them and scaling them up to have a greater impact is where the true transformation happens. In this chapter, we'll explore strategies for maintaining momentum, scaling up from tiny shifts to full adaptation, and the critical role of continued learning and growth in sustaining your habits over the long term.

Maintaining Momentum

Maintaining the momentum of your new habits is essential for long-term success. Outlined below are key strategies in a brief format:

Regular Reviews : Schedule weekly or monthly reviews to assess progress and adjust as needed.

Visual Reminders: Use visual cues like post-it notes or digital reminders to keep your habits top of mind.

Accountability Partners: Share your goals with a trusted friend or mentor for regular check-ins and support.

Scaling Up : From Tiny Shifts to Full Adaptation

Scaling up your habits involves gradually increasing their scope and integrating them into broader routines. This process allows you to build on the foundation of your tiny habit shifts and expand them into more impactful and comprehensive practices. Here's how to effectively scale up your habits:

Incremental Increases

Gradually extend the time or effort dedicated to your habits. Small, consistent increments prevent overwhelm and make the expansion more manageable. This approach ensures that you build on your progress without overloading yourself, allowing the habit to grow naturally.

Example 1 : Exercise Routine

If you started with a five-minute daily workout, gradually increase the duration by a minute or two each week. Over time, this incremental increase will lead to a full 30-minute routine that feels attainable and sustainable.

Example 2 : Reading Goals

If your initial habit was to read for 10 minutes each day, slowly increase this time to 15, 20, or even 30 minutes. This gradual extension allows you to build endurance and integrate the habit more deeply into your daily routine.

Compound Habits

Combine small habits into more comprehensive routines. This technique, known as habit stacking, leverages the foundation of your existing habits to create a more robust and integrated practice. By linking multiple habits together, you can create a powerful routine that addresses multiple areas of improvement simultaneously.

Example 1 : Morning Routine

If you've established habits of meditating for five minutes and reading for 10 minutes, combine these into a single morning routine. Add other beneficial activities, such as stretching or journaling, to create a comprehensive start to your day.

Example 2: Professional Development

Combine habits such as checking industry news, practicing a new skill, and networking online into a daily professional development routine. This compounded approach ensures you address various aspects of your career growth in a cohesive manner.

Setting Bigger Goals

Set more ambitious goals as your confidence and capability grow. Once you've successfully integrated and maintained your initial habits, challenge yourself with larger objectives. Bigger goals push you to expand your horizons and achieve more significant milestones.

Example 1 : Career Milestones

If your initial goal was to network with one new person each week, set a more ambitious goal to attend a monthly industry conference or speak at an event. These bigger goals leverage your established networking habit to achieve greater professional visibility and opportunities.

Example 2 : Skill Mastery

If you began by learning a new skill for 15 minutes a day, set a goal to complete a certification course or teach the skill to others. This ambitious step builds on your foundational habit and drives deeper expertise and mastery.

New Techniques for Sustaining and Scaling Habits

To enhance your ability to sustain and scale habits effectively, consider incorporating these advanced techniques into your routine:

1. Habit Layering

Habit Layering involves integrating new habits with established routines, enhancing the likelihood of sustained practice over time.

Implementing Habit Layering:

Identify a Stable Habit : Choose a habit that is already well-established in your daily routine.

Layer a New Habit : Introduce a new habit that complements or builds upon the existing one. For example, if you already have a morning exercise routine, layer on a habit of meditation immediately afterward.

Gradually Increase Complexity: As the layered habits become more ingrained, gradually increase their complexity or duration. This incremental approach ensures steady growth without overwhelming yourself.

2. Environmental Design

Environmental Design focuses on adjusting your surroundings to support the maintenance and growth of your habits.

Designing Your Environment:

Minimize Distractions : Organize your workspace or living area to minimize distractions that could derail your habits.

Easy Access : Place tools, resources, or reminders for your habits in visible and accessible locations. This makes it easier to engage in your habits without unnecessary effort.

Create a Supportive Space : Designate a physical space that is conducive to the practice of your habits. For instance, if you're learning a new language, create a study corner with language materials and comfortable seating.

3. Behavioral Triggers

Behavioral Triggers are specific cues or events that prompt the initiation of your new habits, making them a natural part of your daily routine.

Setting Effective Triggers

Identify Existing Behaviors : Identify existing behaviors or routines that naturally occur throughout your day. These can serve as effective triggers for your new habits.

Associate with Triggers: Link your new habit with these triggers consistently. For example, if you want to develop a habit of drinking more water, associate it with your morning coffee routine.

Reinforce Associations : Reinforce the association between triggers and habits until the new behavior becomes automatic and integrated into your routine.

4. Gamification

Gamification adds game-like elements to habit formation, making it more engaging and motivating.

Applying Gamification

Points or Rewards System : Create a points system or reward structure for completing habit-related tasks. For instance, earn points for each day you practice your habit consistently.

Use Habit Tracking Apps : Utilize apps or tools that turn habit tracking into a game, where you earn rewards or badges for achieving milestones.

Social Competition : Compete with friends, family, or colleagues who are also working on developing new habits. This social element can provide additional motivation and accountability.

5. Visualization Techniques

Visualization Techniques involve mentally rehearsing the practice and benefits of your new habits to enhance their effectiveness.

Practicing Visualization

Daily Visualization : Set aside a few minutes daily to mentally rehearse yourself performing your new habits successfully. Focus on the specific actions and positive outcomes associated with these habits.

Emphasize Positive Feelings : Visualize the feelings of satisfaction, accomplishment, and progress that come with practicing your habits consistently.

Prepare for Challenges : Use visualization to mentally prepare for potential challenges or obstacles that may arise in maintaining your habits. Visualizing yourself overcoming these challenges can increase your resilience and determination.

By integrating these advanced techniques—habit layering, environmental design, behavioral triggers, gamification, and visualization—into your habit formation process, you can significantly enhance your ability to sustain and scale your habits effectively. These methods not only reinforce your determination but also enhance the journey towards achieving your goals, making it more pleasurable and rewarding.

What We Discovered ?

Sustaining and scaling habits requires a combination of regular assessment, strategic integration, and innovative techniques. By maintaining momentum, incrementally increasing your efforts, and leveraging advanced strategies like habit layering, environmental design, behavioral triggers, gamification, and visualization, you can ensure that your habits not only endure but also grow in impact. The journey to professional excellence is dynamic, and your ability to adapt and evolve is key to long-term success. Keep pushing forward, and remember that each small step contributes to your overall growth and achievement.

Did You Know?

Studies from University College London have shown that the likelihood of sticking to a new habit increases by 55% when the habit is tied to a specific time and place. This underscores the importance of environmental cues in sustaining and scaling habits effectively.

Conclusion : Ongoing Journey to Professional Excellence

As we reach the conclusion of our journey through tiny habit shifts and their profound impact on professional excellence, it's essential to reflect on the path ahead. The journey continues beyond this point; it's an endless process of growth, learning, and adaptation. Let's explore how to embrace continuous improvement, maintain a long-term vision for career success, and stay motivated and inspired.

Embracing Continuous Improvement

1. Commitment to Lifelong Learning

Professional excellence is not a destination but a continuous journey. Stay curious and committed to learning new skills, acquiring knowledge, and evolving with your industry.

- **Adopt a Growth Mindset :** Accept challenges as opportunities for development. Treat failures as educational moments instead of setbacks.

- **Seek Feedback :** Routinely seek out feedback from supervisors, peers, and mentors. Use this feedback constructively to refine your habits and improve your performance.

- **Invest in Education :** Take advantage of workshops, courses, and professional development opportunities. Staying updated with the latest trends and technologies in your field will keep you competitive and innovative.

Long-Term Vision for Career Success

1. Setting and Revisiting Goals

Your professional goals should evolve as you grow. Consistently reassess and update your goals to align with your ambitions and the shifting landscape of your field.

- **Define Clear Milestones** : Split your long-term aspirations into smaller, achievable targets. This makes the journey less overwhelming and more manageable.

- **Reflect and Adapt** : Periodically reflect on your progress and achievements. Be adaptable in adjusting your goals when presented with new insights and experiences.

- **Balance Short-Term and Long-Term Planning** : While it's essential to focus on immediate tasks and goals, never lose sight of your long-term vision. Balance your efforts to ensure sustained progress toward your ultimate career aspirations.

Staying Motivated and Inspired

1. Cultivating Intrinsic Motivation

Find joy and purpose in your work. Intrinsic motivation, driven by personal satisfaction and a sense of accomplishment, is far more sustainable than external rewards.

- **Connect with Your Purpose** : Regularly remind yourself why you chose your profession and what you love about it. This connection to your purpose will fuel your passion and dedication.

- **Celebrate Small Wins** : Celebrate and recognize all your achievements, no matter how small. This boosts morale and promotes positive habits.

- **Surround Yourself with Positivity** : Engage with a supportive community of like-minded professionals. Cultivating positive relationships and having a strong support system can significantly increase your motivation.

2. Keeping Inspiration Alive

Inspiration can come from various sources. Stay open to new ideas and perspectives that can ignite your passion and creativity.

- **Read Widely :** Explore books, articles, and thought pieces outside your immediate field. Diverse perspectives can spark innovative ideas and approaches.

- **Attend Conferences and Networking Events :** Network with industry leaders and peers to keep inspired and aware of the latest trends in your field.

- **Mentorship and Coaching :** Seek out mentors who inspire you and can provide guidance. Equally, mentoring others can bring inspiration and facilitate personal development.

Final Thoughts

The path to professional excellence through tiny habit shifts is an ongoing journey, one marked by continuous improvement, adaptability, and resilience. It's a journey that doesn't end with the completion of this book; rather, it begins anew with every small step you take.

Continuous Improvement

At the heart of this journey is the principle of continuous improvement. This means always seeking ways to refine your skills, enhance your knowledge, and optimize your habits.It includes a lifelong dedication to learning, where every experience presents an opportunity for development. This mindset keeps you agile in the face of new challenges and prepares you to seize opportunities as they arise. Continuous improvement isn't about dramatic changes but about making consistent, incremental progress that compounds over time, leading to significant advancements in your professional capabilities.

Embracing Lifelong Learning

Embracing lifelong learning is crucial in a world that is constantly evolving. Industries transform, new technologies emerge, and best practices evolve. Staying competitive and up-to-date necessitates ongoing education and skill building. This can be through formal education, professional development courses, or even self-study. Reading widely, attending workshops, and engaging with thought leaders in your field can provide new insights and inspire innovative approaches. Lifelong learning ensures that you remain at the forefront of your profession, ready to adapt to changes and lead with confidence.

Maintaining a Clear Vision for Your Career

Having a defined career direction is essential. This vision serves as your North Star, guiding your efforts and keeping you focused on your long-term goals. It involves setting specific, measurable, attainable, relevant, and time-bound (SMART) goals that align with your career aspirations. Regularly revisit and revise these goals to reflect your evolving ambitions and the changing landscape of your industry. A clear vision helps you prioritize your efforts, ensuring that each tiny habit shift you make is aligned with your broader objectives. It gives you direction and a sense of purpose, adding meaning to your professional experience.

Staying Motivated and Inspired

Staying motivated and inspired is vital for sustaining your efforts over the long haul. Motivation can wane, and setbacks are inevitable, but maintaining a strong sense of purpose can help you persevere. Cultivating intrinsic motivation—finding joy and fulfillment in the work itself—can sustain you through challenging times. This involves connecting deeply with your reasons for pursuing your career, whether it's a passion for the work, a desire to make a positive impact, or the pursuit of personal growth. Additionally, seek inspiration from various sources—mentors, peers, literature, and even outside your immediate field. Engaging with a community of like-minded professionals can provide support, encouragement, and fresh perspectives, keeping your passion alive and your creativity flowing.

Each Small Step Matters

Remember, each small step you take contributes to your long-term growth and professional fulfillment. Tiny habit shifts, while seemingly minor on their own, accumulate to produce substantial changes. These small, consistent efforts build upon one another, leading to significant transformations over time. It's the principle of compound interest applied to personal development—small, regular investments in your habits yield exponential returns in your professional life. Celebrate these small victories, as they are the building blocks of your larger success.

The Importance of Adaptability and Resilience

Adaptability and resilience are key traits that will support you on this journey. In the ever-shifting professional world, the ability to adapt, pivot as needed, and recover from setbacks is vital. Resilience enables you to bounce back from failures and continue striving towards your goals, while adaptability allows you to stay relevant and responsive to industry trends and changes. By cultivating these traits, you ensure that you can navigate the ups and downs of your career with grace and determination.

Keep Pushing Forward

Persist, stay curious, and strive for excellence without pause. Progressing to professional excellence is a marathon, not a sprint. It requires perseverance, dedication, and a relentless pursuit of improvement. Stay curious about your field, always asking questions and seeking new knowledge. Curiosity drives innovation and keeps you engaged in your work. Strive for excellence in everything you do, holding yourself to high standards and continually seeking ways to enhance your performance. This commitment to excellence will set you apart and propel you towards your career goals.

The Transformative Power of Tiny Habit Shifts

Your dedication to tiny habit shifts will lead to significant and lasting transformation in your professional life. These shifts may start small, but their impact grows as they become ingrained in your daily routine. Over time, they will shape your behaviors, influence your outcomes, and ultimately define your professional success. Embrace this journey with enthusiasm and confidence, knowing that each small change you make brings you closer to your full potential. The transformation may be gradual, but it is profound and enduring, leading to a fulfilling and successful professional life.

TINY HABIT SHIFTS

In conclusion, the path to professional excellence is a continuous journey of self-improvement, learning, and growth. By embracing tiny habit shifts, maintaining a clear vision, staying motivated, and being adaptable, you can achieve remarkable success. Each step you take, no matter how small, is a step towards realizing your professional aspirations. Keep moving forward with curiosity and a commitment to excellence, and watch as your dedication transforms your professional life in meaningful and lasting ways.

Wishing you all the best on the Journey to "Tiny Habit Shifts"

Dear Reader,

Thank you for taking the time to read "Tiny Habits Shifts : A Step-by-step Guide to Building Good Habits and Developing Atomic Habits for Personal Transformation." Your feedback is incredibly valuable to me, and I would love to hear your thoughts on this book. If you found the insights and strategies helpful, please consider leaving a review on the platform where you purchased it. Your reviews not only help me improve but also assist other readers in discovering the benefits of this book. Additionally, I welcome any suggestions or ideas you have for future topics. Your support and input are greatly appreciated and will help me continue to provide valuable content. Thank you for being a part of this journey!

Warm regards,

Sean Harper.

Here are the top 10 facts related to habits:

1. Habit Formation Time Varies :

- The time it takes to form a new habit varies widely among individuals, with research from University College London indicating that it can take anywhere from 18 to 254 days, with an average of 66 days to solidify a new habit.

2. Habit Loop Components :

-Charles Duhigg's theory in 'The Power of Habit' outlines habits as having three parts: the cue (trigger), the routine (behavior), and the reward (benefit achieved).

3. Automaticity Threshold :

- A study in the European Journal of Social Psychology found that behavior becomes more automatic and requires less conscious effort after consistent repetition, with the brain building stronger neural pathways for the habit.

4. Impact on Brain Structure :

- Research shows that habits can physically alter brain structure, specifically strengthening the connections between neurons in the basal ganglia, an area of the brain associated with habit formation and automatic behaviors.

5. Keystone Habits :

- Some habits, known as keystone habits, can spark positive changes in multiple areas of life. For example, regular exercise can improve eating habits, increase productivity, and reduce stress.

6. The Power of Small Changes :

- James Clear, author of "Atomic Habits," emphasizes that making small, incremental changes can lead to significant long-term improvements, a concept known as the 1% rule.

7. Environment Influence :

- The formation of habits is greatly impacted by your surroundings. Modifying your surroundings to remove friction for good habits and increase friction for bad ones can significantly affect your behavior.

8. Cue-Routine-Reward Habit Loop :

-According to MIT researchers, they discovered the neurological mechanism behind the habit loop, detailing how cues prompt routines that end with rewards, strengthening this loop in the brain.

9. Willpower as a Finite Resource :

-Research indicates that willpower can tire similarly to how a muscle fatigues. Thus, creating habits that require less conscious effort can help conserve willpower for more critical decisions.

10. Habit Tracking Increases Success :

- Research indicates that tracking habits increases the likelihood of success. Keeping a log or using an app to monitor progress can provide motivation and accountability.

These points emphasize how habits, with their complexity and influence, play a critical role in personal and professional progress.